HOW TO BE HEALED
FROM SICKNESS & DISEASES THROUGH CHRIST

MARK ASEMOTA

MARYLAND LONDON TORONTO SIDNEY NEW DELHI

Copyright © 2016 by Mark Asemota

All rights reserved. No part of this publication may be reproduced, distributed, or transmitted in any form or by any means, including photocopying, recording, or other electronic or mechanical methods, without the prior written permission of the publisher, except in the case of brief quotations embodied in critical reviews and certain other noncommercial uses permitted by copyright law. For permission requests, write to the publisher, addressed "Attention: Permissions Coordinator," at the address below.

Mark Asemota House of Publishing
13203 Wonderland way,
Germantown, MD 20874

Ordering Information:
Quantity sales. Special discounts are available on quantity purchases by corporations, associations, and others Barnes & Nobles, Amazon or visit www.ingramspark.com,
How to be Healed From Sickness and Diseases.net and any other Major bookstore all over the world

Printed in the United States of America

ISBN 978-0-9891629-4-4

The main category of the book —Religion—Other category. Christianity - Healing

DEDICATION

To my father H. Asemota who first told me about miracle, to my mother Elizabeth Asemota who took me to witness my first miracle, and to Yemisi Foluhi who brought me into miracle through the gospel of our Lord Jesus Christ.

What Others Are Saying About

HOW TO BE HEALED FROM SICKNESS AND DISEASES THROUGH CHRIST

A must read revelation by Pastor Mark. The Power of Penticost is to impact and to bring about healing of people in the present age

DR. FEMI ALABI
BISHOP ELECT AND FOUNDER BETHEL OF PRAISE MINISTRIES
CHIEF VOLUNTEER OFFICER -
ALPHA COMMUNITY DEVELOPMENT CORPORATION

Spiritually intelligent and divinely ordained to bring hope and life. Carefully written guidlines to whole cure and restoration

APOSTLE JOHN KING HILL
AUTHOR OF MYSTERIES OF HEAVEN &
HOST OF POWER&GLORY WORLDWIDE
TELEVISION BROADCAST.

I would reccommend this book to anyone dealing with health issies and not understanding why they haven't been healed

REV. STEVIE OKAURU
AUTHOR, ORACLE OF GOD DAILY DEVOTIONAL
PRESIDENT & FOUNDER ORACLE OF GOD INT'L MINISTRIES

Foreword

Bishop LaDonna Osborn, D.Min.

Not all books even all great books, come as a voice from above, but I feel this one does. From the moment you turn to the first page, it is like turning on a faucet of the love of God for the healing of his children. As you read further it is like holding a glass filled with profound truth on healing.

This book is an outstanding contribution to the ministry of healing. Pastor Mark, with simplicity of language skips over fruitless theological jargon to deliver healing principles that make Gospel truth embracing and usable for all. This book is no doubt a work borne out of meditation, experience and prayer. Every chapter is lively and rich, and overall, the book can be summarized by Paul's exclamation *"O the depth of the riches both of the wisdom and knowledge of God."* While deep truths are expounded, the delivery is simple and the outcome is powerful.

Here is a book for those who are in need of healing, and for every pastor, missionary and Christian who insist on wellness. The reader will close this book with a greater understanding of ministry of healing provided by Christ..

Acknowledgments

Foremost thanks go to the Lord Jesus who made healing a reality and God almighty who inspired the words written here.

Throughout the process of writing this book, many individuals played significant roles not only to bring it to completion but in delivering it as an effective timely tool. Special thanks to my energetic and loving wife Obi Okafor Asemota who in addition to her continuing support helped tremendously in the editorials. And special thanks to Dr John Hill whose persisting nudge to go on, and tireless insight into the subject of healing helping completing this book. I would love to thank Dr Bassey Efiok who also helped advance this book by offering comments, proofreading and presenting current viable option for production.

I am deeply grateful to Pastor Johnson Olatunde a man of prayer and painstaking attention to detail who also helped in proofreading and praying.

And to Pastor Femi and Philomena Alabi, I am speechless. Your big heart and altruism is noticeable and adorable. Thanks very much.

Last but not the least: I ask forgiveness of all those who have been with me over the course of the years and whose names I have failed to mention." May God almighty reward your good works.

HOW TO BE HEALED
FROM SICKNESS & DISEASES
THROUGH CHRIST

CONTENTS

INTRODUCTION . . . . *ix*

PROLOGUE . . . . *x*

CHAPTER 1
WHAT GOD SAYS ABOUT YOUR HEALING   PAGE 1

- What has a serpent got to do with it? *3*
- Your Disease and sickness expired like
  Pills in a bottle *6*
- Mass Miracle at Marah *11*
- That Night everything changed *15*
- Prophecy waiting to be fulfilled *20*

CHAPTER 2
WHAT JESUS DID ABOUT YOUR ILLINESS   PAGE 24

- Sympathy or substitution *26*
- When he atoned for your sins, he healed you *28*
- Your sickness is part of what he Carried away *29*
- Jesus Just like Moses *32*
- Even in the grave Jesus is Lord *33*
- If you are saved you are healed *35*
- Sin and sickness same and alike *37*

CHAPTER 3
DISSOLVING DOUBTS   PAGE 38

- Am I in good standing that God is willing to heal me? *40*
- Can my past sin hinder me from being healed? *42*
- What are the sins that can hinder me
  from being healed? *44*
- This sickness runs in my family *46*
- What about Job of old? *47*
- Am already old –this sickness could
  be from God *51*
- If I keep getting healed how am I ever
  Going to die? *52*
- Old age sickness is not of God *53*
- How do I know I am healed when I
  don't feel healed? *55*

CHAPTER 4
FAR-REACHING IMPLICATION OF THE GOSPEL   PAGE 59
OF OUR LORD JESUS

- Do Christians die? Or do they lay down
  their Lives? *60*
- How to lay down our life *62*

CONTENTS CONTINUED

- *Living seventy years or Forever* 63
- *Generational Curse hoax* 65

CHAPTER 5
OVERCOMING HINDRANCES TO YOUR HEALING   PAGE 71

- *Faith in what Jesus has done is the Surefire way to healing* 71
- *Recounting this story will heal you a : confession* .. 73
- *Do not fight the symptoms fight the doubts* 76
- *Mind over matter or the Spirit declaring Rhema* .. 78
- *Fight mentality, not a victim Of mentality* 79
- *Your faith is highly developed in Doctors What are you going to do about it?* 80
- *Little foxes, short circuit the power Of healing* ... 82
- *Demons and false faith: hindrances to healing and how to deal with the demons* 84
- *Electric Properties of the anointing of Healing* ... 86
- *Jesus Ministers higher volts too* 88
- *If donkey talks, and handkerchiefs heal!* 89

CHAPTER 6
TESTIMONIES OF HEALING THROUGH THE WORD   PAGE 95

- *Fibroid Disappears during the teaching of the word.* ... 96
- *She chose to stay and her Cataract was healed* 97
- *Skin cancer healed after word radiation* 98
- *How God healed me of chronic illness Several years ago* 99

CHAPTER 7
CONCLUSION: FIVE ESSENTIAL TO MIRACULOUS   PAGE 101
          HEALING

- *Prevenient visions* 102
- *Planted visions* 103
- *Professed visions* 104
- *Persuaded of visions or promise* 105
- *Praises to performance of miracle* 106

HEALING SCRIPTURE FOR MEDITATION   109

Introduction:
Why I wrote this book?

I wrote this book because I was instructed by the Lord to write it. It is presented in a concise and incisive yet very simple manner because I became very concerned about people who are suffering from one sickness. I wanted to be able to put something of self-help for healing into their hand. I am excited about writing the book because over a period of time the Lord has shown me some very useful secret to divine healing. I know that if people could get hold of these truths they would as soon begin to receive their healing as in bible days.

The *words concerning the work of Jesus* are the building bonds of divine healing. Except to the spiritually undiscerning that considers such truth too abstract, the word is as tangible as the work of Jesus. If believed with the heart and affirmed through the word of mouth prayerfully it will bring miracles just as when Jesus spoke the word in person.

The Word of God is the language of the spirit. The word of God is a programming language. It is language to the human body as programming language is to computers. Computer only understands *machine language*. They understand nothing else. When these machine languages are fed into it, the computer responds and carries out command. So is the human body; it only understands the *Word of God*. When the Word is fed into the human spirit, condition of healing is effected.

This book is essentially the W*ord languages* to be fed into the seeker's spirit so that the command of healing can be carried out. I thank The Holy Spirit not only for bringing these truth to you but also in highlighting them to the end that you believe with the heart, affirm them with the mouth and experience the power in your body.

Pastor Mark Asemota

> *Go, stand and speak in the temple*
> *to the people all the words of this life.*
> *Act 5:20*

Prologue

The works of Jesus Christ concerning you and me can be summed up simply in two words '*eternal life*'. Eternal life is the *sine qua non* of the power of God in the new man. Jesus spoke these words: *and lifting up His eyes to heaven, He said, "Father, the hour has come; glorify your Son, that the Son may glorify you, even as you gave Him authority over all flesh, that to all whom you have given Him, He may give eternal life.* ^{John 3:15}

If a man received eternal life then he has received all that Christ came to give him. As important as this truth is, the meaning of the word eternal life is constantly being misunderstood. The meaning has been considerably shrunk in some quarter as to be of no benefit to us this present time.

Some have concluded that eternal life is in heaven after death. If eternal life is only in heaven after death, it is certainly of no importance to us here. It would need to be received only after death. However, the bible said, *that you may know that you have eternal life* – this is not something of the future. We have that life now. The scripture clearly said that we have eternal life - now and today, if we believe in Jesus Christ.

People have also described eternal life as a long endless existence in the hereafter. Again this is could be misleading. Let us accept for a moment that eternal life is an endless existence. The big question is, what benefit is a long boring poverty-riddled and disease-stricken existence? Certainly that cannot be all about eternal life. Besides, both the saints and sinners have endless existence hereafter: sinners an endless death and the saints an endless life. Eternal life offers much more.

Eternal life is the very type of life Jesus has. It is the type of life that God has. It is called 'Zoe'. Plant has a type of life different from animal. The ordinary man has a type life different from that of God. The God kind of life is called 'Zoe' and it is different and superior to all other types of life.

This is the life Jesus died to give us. We have the God kind of life and that is what eternal life mean. God kind of life. Of course it is endless and transcends this present world, but the essence of this life is that it is not subject to death, disease, sin or poverty.

Plants, as well as animals are subject to disease and death, and even the angelic life is subject to sin. But the *life of God,* that the *English language* frantically and arduously defined as eternal life is neither subject to disease or sickness. That is why I said earlier that if we received eternal life we have perfect health.

We are therefore sharing in the God kind of life. We have been inducted into the class of beings with divine nature through Jesus Christ. Apostle Peter said, *through the work of Jesus God has given us his very great and precious promises, so that through them we may participate in the divine nature, having escaped the corruption in the world caused by evil desires.* 2 Peter 1:3

It is equally difficult to even comprehend that we have the divine nature as we are. Nevertheless, this is what eternal life is about.

Another way to look at it is to know that because the first man, Adam died, the ordinary man or woman is not really living. Mankind is dying progressively. We have people, everywhere at different levels of decomposition. That is why people get old, that is also why people get less healthy with age and of course that is why people eventually die physically. But when we receive eternal life death is reversed, we begin to live for the very first time since we are born. Remember that Health is life; Healing is life; Prosperity and deliverance from sin is life. When we received eternal life we are said to be born again. It is not only a hope or ticket to heaven but a vital working life that swallows up sin, sickness and disease. <u>If only we were told the whole truth then the whole truth will be actively working in our lives. The benefit of salvation is truncated by the limitation of the instruction we received at birth.</u>

In the following chapters, this *very life* will be unfolded as it pertains to healing. It is such a beautiful and powerful life. Again, we already have eternal life when we received Christ. Some Christians are always trying to get something from God when in fact they should be praying for the ability to see what they have already been given. Like Apostle Paul prayed, *that the God of our Lord Jesus Christ, the glorious Father, may give us the Spirit of wisdom and revelation, that the eyes of our heart may be enlightened in order that we may know the hope to which he has called us, the riches of his glorious inheritance in his holy people, and his incomparably great power toward us who believe.*

Apostle Paul said *that this power is the same as the mighty strength he exerted when he raised Christ from the dead and seated him at his right hand in the heavenly realms, far above all rule and authority, power and dominion, and every name that is invoked, not only in the present age but also in the one to come.* $^{Eph\ 1:17-22}$

If you have not received Jesus Christ into your life then the first step in maximizing this gospel is to receive him now so that this eternal life can be at work in you-. If on the other hand you have received him then you should pray that the spirit of wisdom and revelation should be at work in you.

The following pages blaze forth the essence of this life. It will show you how to engage this eternal life either by yourself or in cooperating with a minister to receive your healing. By the time you are done reading this book prayerfully you will no longer have problem with faith to get healed. No matter what the problem is the power of God revealed in this book will bring healing and health to you.

*Life is a tapestry: we are the warp; angels are
The weft and God is the weaver. Only the
Weaver sees the whole design* – Eileen Elias Freeman

CHAPTER 1

WHAT GOD SAYS ABOUT YOUR HEALING

SOMEONE ONCE SAID that *'where the will of God is unknown, perfect faith is impossible'*. A person cannot have more faith than his or her understanding of the will of God. The will of God in the case of healing is what God has declared concerning healing. Faith cannot be based on suppositions, theories or vague hope. Once we understand what God says about a subject, faith is activated in our hearts. It is therefore important that we understand what God is saying concerning our healing. God made His position known concerning sicknesses and diseases through his excellent master communicating abilities. Throughout the Old and New Testament, God has made His will to heal so clear that even a fool will not misunderstand it. When we know the truth about the will of God concerning sicknesses the truth produces conviction. We then come under the power of these convictions. Conviction is tenacious, Conviction is transforming, Conviction, is what truth does in us. It makes stubborn faith out of stubbles. It causes us to lay a firm unyielding grip on God's promise until the divine healing power is set in motion. God communicates his will on healing through remarkable stories in the Old Testament books which brings such convictions as we speak. The prophecies, the Psalms and the Law of Moses communicates his will.

The bible said, "These are the words that I spake unto you, while I was yet with you, that all things must be fulfilled which were written in the Law of Moses and in the Prophets and in the Psalms concerning me." Luke 24:44

The Prophets and the Psalms contain stories and through these stories, which are called **'shadows or types'** we are able to know whether our present expectation of healing is valid or not. Types or shadows are ways God foretell the work of Jesus Christ.

*For the law having a **shadow** of good things to come, and not the very image of the things... Heb. 10:1*

One of such shadows is the story of how the Israelites were beaten by snakes in the wilderness and how God cured them by commanding Moses to erect a serpent of Brass.

What has a serpent got to do with it?

And Moses made a serpent of brass, and put it upon a pole, and it came to pass, that if a serpent had bitten any man, when he beheld the serpent of brass, he lived. Numbers 21:9 (- King James Bible "Authorized Version", Cambridge Edition)

Although God is not responsible for Israel's sin, He orchestrated this event and wove a prophecy into the story. This story is of significance to a future event about healing; here the Israelites sinned against God and God sent snakes to bite them, Moses Cried to God for healing and God designed a solution; The solution is the *serpent on the pole that heals*. It was their point of contact for the release of the healing power of God. He said if they look at the Serpent of brass they would not die of the venom of the snakes. Secondly, the snakes will not bite them anymore. It worked! Israel was healed.

The serpent of brass was a prophecy concerning Jesus Christ healing us through the cross. The way Moses lifted the snake of brass is the same way Jesus is lifted up on the cross and whosoever look onto Jesus receives healing and protection from diseases and sickness.

"As Moses lifted up the serpent in the wilderness, even so must the Son of Man be lifted up; so that whoever believes in Him will have eternal life...John 3:14

Throughout the Old Testament portion of the bible you will find so many stories like this illustrating future event, which as I said earlier are Called types or shadow; *A* pre-ordained event; a shadow of some sort cast by God in the Old testament portion of the bible that gives us a picture of what is to happen in the new testament. What happened here provides a ground for the expectation of miraculous healing. When the snakes bit the Israelites, they looked at the serpent of brass on the pole and they were healed. Likewise today, we can be healed if we would only look at Jesus Christ on the cross by apprehending his significance on that cross.

This Serpent of brass *'shadow',* help us see differently, especially for people who seems to think that the bible is a fable or a random collection of literature. They will begin to have much deeper appreciation for the Work of Jesus on the Cross, as they are able to see that stories in the bible like this are fore-ordained, pre-meditated and organized events calculated toward a particular end. In this case it is healing. It is evident that whatever the serpent on the pole was to Israel, Jesus Christ and the cross is to us. Therefore, we have the right to expect healing today when bitten by sickness as the Israelites had when bitten by the serpent.

The Connection

This account actually puzzled me as a young believer. I just could not make the connection between a devilish frightening snake and a holy

Jesus. But it is simple. God was saying *'look at the snake that bit you, I have defeated it.*

Now it may not make a lot of sense to them except that they were healed. This is because God is speaking to us through their story and not to them. It makes sense to us when we consider Jesus on the cross; we see that when he went to the Cross he took sin and sickness with him and nailed them to the cross. Snake is symbolic of sin and temptation. So Jesus became sin.

God made him who had no sin to be sin for us,...
... God sending his own Son in the likeness of sinful flesh, and for sin, condemned sin in the flesh..
2 Cor. 5:21, Rom. 8:3

On the cross, Jesus epitomizes the symbol of sin. he had become sin for us. he embodied our sins and sickness. Now Jesus on the cross even as the serpent of brass was on the pole signifies the defeat of sin and sickness because sin and sickness is crucified. There is our victory as the Israelites' victory. Not only were they cured but were also immune from the venom of the snakebites they suffered.

This Jesus on the cross-had become sin in order that he might nail it to the cross.

The bible said, God sending his own Son in the likeness of sinful flesh, and for sin, condemned sin in the flesh... Romans 8:3

All we like sheep have gone astray; we have turned everyone to his own way; and the lord hath laid on him the iniquity of us all...Isa. 53:6

When we think of the cross let us not just see Jesus on the cross. Let us see our infirmities on the cross as well, Jesus having taken them on. And when he was nailed to that cross just as the serpent of brass was nailed to that pole our disease and sickness was nailed with him. We can look at the cross and say, '*there goes all my sickness and disease!*'

...Having canceled out the certificate of debt consisting of decrees against us, which was hostile to us; and He has taken it out of the way, having nailed it to the cross. Col. 2:14 (New American Standard Bible)

Your Disease and sickness expired like Pills in a bottle

Problems never last forever. Problems are like pill; they do expire. You remember how you look at the bottle and the expiration date says, *expired!* What do you do? You toss the bottle with the pills into the trash bin.

That is what happens in the days of Moses when he confronted Pharaoh. The period stipulated for Israel's slavery had simply expired. 400 years had passed. God had said to Abraham that his children will be in slavery for 400 years.

God said to Abram, "Know for certain that your descendants will be strangers in a land that is not theirs, where they will be enslaved and oppressed four hundred years." Genesis 15:13

After four-hundred years, their '*slavery pill*' expired and Moses came on the scene. We see the same scenario repeated in Babylon Empire. Jeremiah had prophesied that Israel would be in Babylonian captivity for seventy years.

... *"For thus says the LORD, 'When seventy years have been completed for Babylon, I will visit you and fulfill my good word to you, to bring you back to this place. Jeremiah 29:10 (NIV)*

Again, we see that after seventy-years the *Slavery pill* expired and Daniel came on the scene. Prophet Daniel made the discovery by searching through books; the *slavery pill* had expired; they no longer have to remain in captivity. He knew they only need to remind God of the expiration date and God would deliver them.

"I, Daniel, was perusing the scriptures, counting over the number of years -- as revealed by God to the prophet Jeremiah -- before the successive devastations of Jerusalem would come to an end, namely seventy years." Daniel 9:2

It is good to know that no problem can last forever. Every problem has an expiration date. If we endure, the problem will eventually *expire.* Every problem comes with a tag; to whom, for what, and for how long? For how long refers to the stipulated duration of the problem. So whatever the problem you think you have now; whether you are looking to have a child, or you are suffering from a physical ailment, you must understand that the situation has an expiration date.

What about our problems? Do we sit and wait for a stipulated expiration date to elapse? Well that would be such a great news now. The good news is that for us we are living in the days Jesus called '*acceptable year of the Lord*". If reduced to simple terms means the days in which the problems we are carrying have expired.

..The Spirit of the Lord is upon me (Jesus)... To Proclaim the acceptable year of the Lord...
Isaiah 61:1-2 (Parenthesis added)

This acceptable year is the year of Jubilee. God has said in the days of atonement, which is the year of Jubilee; a proclamation of freedom should be made. This is what Jesus was proclaiming or declaring.

Then shall thou cause the trumpet of the jubilee to sound on the tenth day of the seventh month, in the Day of Atonement shall ye make the trumpet sound throughout all your land.
And ye shall hallow the fiftieth year, and proclaim Liberty throughout all the land unto all the inhabitants thereof; it shall be a jubilee unto you; and ye shall return every man to his possession, and ye shall return every man unto his family...Lev. 25:9-10

Jesus is the atonement. The days of Jesus on earth are the 'Day of Atonement'. Jesus is also the trumpet-sounding priest being a priest himself. He began to sound the trumpet from the beginning of his ministry.

The bible says 'He went to Nazareth, where he had been brought up, and on the Sabbath day he went into the synagogue, as was his custom. He stood up to read, (17) and the scroll of the prophet Isaiah was handed to him. Unrolling it, he found the place where it is written:

(18) "The Spirit of the Lord is on me, because he has anointed me to proclaim good news to the poor. He has sent me to proclaim freedom for the prisoners and recovery of sight for the blind,

to set the oppressed free, to **proclaim the year of the Lord's favor.**' Luke 4:18(NIV)

This year of favor, is the year of freedom; the year of Jubilee. It is also called the year of Sabbath or the acceptable year to God. In that year, all problems whatsoever expire. This is good news for us! Those to whom Jesus spoke, had they known that Jesus was proclaiming their freedom would not have crucified him.

All forms of slavery, bondage to sickness comes to an end at Jubilee. This is what happens at Jubilee. After forty-nine years; (7 years x 7 years of Sabbath) in the fiftieth year all problems they have is considered expired. If you owe anyone it is written off.

And thou shalt number seven Sabbaths of years unto thee, seven times seven years; and the space of the seven Sabbaths of years shall be unto thee forty and nine years.

Then shalt thou cause the trumpet of the jubilee to sound on the tenth [day] of the seventh month, in the Day of Atonement shall ye make the trumpet sound throughout all your land.

And ye shall hallow the fiftieth year, and proclaim liberty throughout [all] the land unto all the inhabitants thereof: it shall be a jubilee unto you; and ye shall return every man unto his possession, and ye shall return every man unto his family....Lev. 25:8-10

If anyone owes, the debt is forgiven, no matter how large or small. If there were any prisoners they were to be set free. This is what makes Jubilee one of most remarkable event in Israel. Those who were fortunate enough to experience Jubilee in their lifetime know what a relief and freedom it brings. As Israel experienced freedom during the year of jubilee, God is also saying through this story or shadow that, we experience freedom from all sickness and diseases through the declaration of Jesus Christ.

This is a great news for us, but the devil makes plain truth very dark and manages to avoid the spotlight as the culprit. He shroud the magnanimity of the work of Christ under the veneer of putrefying lies, petty doctrines, ridiculous arguments. How could he blinded us to the truth that stare at us in the face? How, after God has shed on us His mercy and ushered us into the abundant life we are still stuck on the wayside with the notion of a panhandling God is beyond understanding? Jesus proclamation is a relief for the sick but the enemy continues to distort the truth.

It seems the enemy is doing a far greater work against the truth today than ever before. The man who rejects Jesus is blind, but for us who have accepted him and do not enjoy the fullness of his work it is scandalous. The only faith we really need here is the faith to believe that our problem have expired because it is Jubilee.

*..The Spirit of the Lord is upon me... To Proclaim the acceptable year of the Lord (Jubilee)...Isa **61:1-2***

As believers we don't need the faith to be healed. We need faith to believe that our illness have expired because Jesus have proclaimed the year of freedom (year of expiration of sickness and diseases). It does not matter our crime, our age or who we are, this proclamation is for all and to all who live in the Jubilee. It is our rest; our Sabbath. That is why Jesus healed on

Sabbath and demanded why the daughter of Abraham should be bound on the Sabbath.

And he was teaching in one of the synagogues on the Sabbath. And, behold, there was a woman which had a spirit of infirmity eighteen years, and was bowed together, and could in no wise lift up herself. And when Jesus saw her, he called her to him, and said unto her, Woman, thou art loosed from thine infirmity...Luke 13:12

The true rest

The fiftieth year which is the year of Jubilee is the Sabbath year, and therefore called a year of rest. People talk about rest when they die. But *the true rest is Sabbath.*
This is what the Apostle Paul refers to as our rest; Sabbath is our rest. Jesus came to declare our rest.

We who have believed have entered into our rest...Hebrews 4:3

That *'rest'* starts when Jesus came to proclaim the acceptable year of the Lord; the year of Jubilee. Those that believe him entered it by faith. If we believe this truth we also will enter into our rest from sickness and diseases. This is a weapon in our arsenal; a formidable evidence in the court of law against the devils. This truth about Jubilee as the year of freedom is a key to our healing from all sicknesses and diseases.

Mass Miracle at Marah

Over five million people departed Egypt under Moses. In a period of forty years these people walked through the wilderness and none of them were found to be sick! They had no medical insurance, no hospital, and no first aid kit. They have no need for them!

Then he led the Israelites out; they carried silver and gold, and all of them were healthy and strong. Psalm 105:37 (GNT)

They became a nation of healthy people. Wow! They have not always been like that though, God healed them at Marah. This is the first thing God did when they came out of Egypt after crossing the Red Sea.
When they got to Marah they were extremely thirsty but the water at Marah was bitter. Then Moses cried unto the lord and the Lord gave Moses the healing guideline;

God told him to cut a tree and cast it into the water of Marah. When Moses did the water turned to sweet. Exodus 15:22-24

The water of Marah was made sweet; the people drank and were satisfied. After they drank, not only were they all healed, everyone of them also became immune to sicknesses and diseases. It was a day of a *mass miracle of healing.* Over five million people were healed after drinking the water into which Moses cast the *tree.* The tree is a type of the cross and the water typifies the Holy Spirit. The cross and the Holy Spirit neutralizes the bitterness in our lives and changes the *'chemical composition of our situation'.* Jesus was crucified on the cross (the tree)

Christ hath redeemed us from the curse of the law, being made a curse for us: for it is written, Cursed is every one that hangeth on a tree: Gal 3:13

God is communicating to us by this story that on the cross of Calvary a mass miracle of healing took place in our lives too. Calvary is to us what Marah was to the Israelites. There they were all healed by that tree. At Calvary we were all healed by the cross. What God spoke using the events in their lives; He is also speaking to us today. Apostle Paul says these things are written for our examples. *1 Cor. 10:11*

What is an example? Take for instance a teacher teaching arithmetic in a classroom. He writes a math problem, solved it meticulously showing the students every step of the way how to arrive at the answer; then give them similar ones to solve themselves. The one he solved would be an example. It ensures that the next problem the students encounter they can solve following the example of the teacher. This story here is such examples; that as the Israelites believed in Moses and were healed at Marah, we too should believe in Jesus and be healed at the cross.

He also revealed himself as the exclusive Healer of his people

When they drank the water not only was their thirst satisfied but they got healed of every ailment. This is where and how God declared Himself as their Healer.

....For I am the Lord that heal you. Exodus 15:26

God was saying to them, Healing is my Job. I am God, your physician – literally speaking. God did not say, I am your accountant! He did not say I am your Engineer; I will build your roads. Rather He said I am your physician – the God that healeth thee. God sends His Word and shows us the cross of Jesus Christ as the answer. He does not want humans to interfere with His business of healing.

Why Doctors? I do not mean any offence. I respect Doctors and I believe they are the only hope that people who can enjoy divine healing have. And in some cases God can only get through to some people by medical doctors since this is the only hope they have. In the original will of God however Medical Doctors are not agent of healing. When Adam sinned and became naked he covered himself with leaves. Like the leaves in the Garden of Eden with which Adam covered himself so is curative medicine at its best. It is like a '*patch* up' until men begin to believe God to see the redemption of the Lord.

Sickness is of the devil

God also reveals at Marah that sickness is associated with Egypt. Not Egypt of today but the allegorical Egypt. Once they left Egypt they no longer suffer Egyptian diseases. Some seems to think that sickness is natural or inevitable as long as we are in this world. We know from this story that this is untrue. Sickness is a consequence of where you live (spiritually Rev. 18:4); your territory or with whom you are associated. But in Christ we have been removed to a new place where there is no sickness.

We have been Translated from the Kingdom of darkness unto the Kingdom of his son Jesus (Col 1:13)

Even if we stray away from this new territory in Christ, we can always return and our heavenly Doctor, God, will heal us through faith in His Son, Jesus Christ.

I (God) heal all your diseases. Psalm 103 (Word in parenthesis added)

Know this for a fact. When this truth gets hold of us we would soon do away with the paraphernalia of curative medicine. The best and honest of Doctors will tell you that medical science is an attempt; an approximation. It is a compendium of trial and errors. God expects us to develop our faith until we wholly trust on Him to enjoy our healing. In this scripture, God was unhappy with a King for seeking the physician of this world when he should have called on the Lord.

Though his disease was severe, even in his illness he did not seek help from the LORD, but only from the physicians... Woe to those who go down to Egypt for help,
.. But do not look to the Holy One of Israel, or seek help from the LORD. 2 Chron. 16:12, Isa. 31:1

If we truly develop our faith we will find out that the cross is enough. Because when he went to the cross he permanently destroyed sickness. The cross is an offense to sickness and diseases.

That Night everything changed

For over several days Moses continues to pummel Egypt with terrible plagues when Pharaoh would not let Israel go.

Moreover, the LORD showed great and distressing signs and wonders before our eyes against Egypt, Pharaoh and all his household...Deut. 6:22

God made every drop of water in Egypt turn to blood. And when Pharaoh continues to harden his heart God brought disgusting frogs upon Egypt such that everywhere you look there were frogs. God continues to strike Egypt with one catastrophe after the other. But, despite the horrible blows being dealt to Egypt Pharaoh Hardened his heart *and would not let the people go.* ^{Exo 8:32}

The final straw

The final straw came at the Passover night when God went *'through the land of Egypt on that night, and will strike down all the firstborn in the land of Egypt, both man and beast; and against all the gods of Egypt…'* Exodus 12:12

God commanded Israel to put blood upon their lintel and that when He sees the blood he will Passover.

'The blood shall be a sign for you on the houses where you live; and when I see the blood I will pass over you, and no plague will befall you to destroy you when I strike the land of Egypt…'
Exodus 12:12-13

He will not allow destruction to come to them when He sees the blood. But He would pass on to their Egyptian neighbor and wreak havoc. That was the Passover. The Passover blood pitted God against Egypt but places God behind Israel. Passover is the final blow that decapitated Egypt's principalities and powers. It was the Passover that broke Pharaoh's back bone and broke the slavery chains over Israel.

Because *'At midnight the LORD struck down all the firstborn in the land of Egypt, from the firstborn of Pharaoh who sat on his throne to the firstborn of the captive who was in the dungeon, and all the firstborn of the livestock..Exodus 12:29*

God destroyed the authority and power responsible for Israel's misery. Passover exterminated Israel tormentors. And overnight Israel became a nation. A free nation overnight- A rich nation and a healthy nation! It was the night everything changed.

And he brought them forth with silver and gold; and there was not one feeble person among his tribes. ...Psalm 107:37

Here again is another glaring revelation of Jesus in this Passover story. It is not difficult to see that JESUS is the Passover lamb. What happened that dreadful night in Egypt is the same thing that happened when Jesus was slain. That was the night God destroyed principalities and power. God told every family in Israel to take a Passover lamb and put the blood of the sacrificed lamb on their doors. Jesus is today our Passover lamb.

For Christ our Passover also has been sacrificed... 1 Cor. 5:7

Therefore when Pilate heard these words, he brought Jesus out, and sat down on the judgment seat at a place called The Pavement, but in Hebrew, Gabbatha. Now it was the day of preparation for the Passover; it was about the sixth hour. And he said to the Jews, "Behold, your King!"... John 19:13

The allegorical Egypt represents hell. Jesus shed-blood gave him access to hell. And once in hell he defeated principalities and power. It is imperative that the principalities of Egypt is completely destroyed in order to guarantee the total deliverance of Israel. God had to break Egypt's Powers from off Israel. This He did by the Passover. If God had not taken away the authority and power of Egypt, she would have remained a perpetual reproach to Israel. In the same way, if we are healed once the enemy can strike again unless God destroy the authority of the enemy once and for all time.

That is what happened when Jesus shed his passover blood. As God passed through the land of Egypt destroying heads of families at the Passover night, so, Jesus also passed through hell defeating the host of darkness when he died on the cross. Here is important scripture that reveals this fact;

When he ascended on high he led a host of captives, and he gave gifts to men. In saying, "He ascended," what does it mean but that he had also descended into the lower regions, the earth? 10 He who descended is the one who also ascended far above all the heavens, that he might fill all things.) Eph. 4:8-10 (NIV)

"For thou wilts not leave my soul in hell; neither wilt thou suffer thine Holy One to see corruption....

Here we see that Jesus had to pass through Hell to guarantee our ultimate victory. It is important that Jesus go to hell to defeat the powers in hell because hell is the head-quarter of sin and sickness. Sin gives birth to sicknesses, diseases and death. As Israel could not be permanently free without the Passover Night so we cannot be free without Jesus as the Passover either. By the Passover therefore, Jesus took away both our suffering and our sufferers. He is our Passover Lamb who took away our suffering by dealing with those who afflict us. If our sickness must permanently disappear it is imperative that the progenitor of sickness is stopped forever.

The Man from Tampa

A man came to us in Tampa, Florida, when we went to Tampa for a revival meeting. He is a humble and good believer. He is the pastor of one of the mega churches around. He knelt down to ask for prayers. He said he used to be a member of a deadly African cult. He confessed that, although he had found Jesus Christ, he continues to live in fear. He was afraid because according to him those who deserted the cult had met with terrible death.

Can you relate? Well, the good news however is that Jesus Christ defeated Satan's demonic power-houses the *night of Passover*. We told the man he had nothing to be afraid of. No matter how powerful the demon may be they are already defeated. That is what killing the firstborn of the Egyptian is all about. It means destroying the foremost powers. Jesus made a show of them when he got to that dungeon of hell.

When He had disarmed the rulers and authorities, He made a public display of them, having triumphed over them through Him. Col 2:15 (NASB)

This man's fear of his former cult is unfounded. He is like an Israelite who although had long gone from Egypt having crossed the red sea and seen the soldiers drown yet continued to look over his shoulders for fear of the defunct Egyptians.

Prophecy waiting to be fulfilled

Our healing is a prophecy (divinely inspired utterance of the will of God) waiting to be fulfilled. We do see that not only does God foretell His will to heal through the stories He also spoke through the mouths and writing of His Prophets about His will to heal. When God pronounces a thing through His prophets that thing must surely come to pass. Like every other prophecy God has already pre-determined healing for us. There are over 300 prophecies in the bible pointing to Jesus. Many of the prophecies have been fulfilled. The following healing prophecies are already fulfilled and are waiting to be claimed by individuals.

Those who believe the word of the Lord with expectation to experience His healing power will see these prophecies materialized in their lives, even in our time and generation.

"For truly I say to you, until heaven and earth pass away, not the smallest letter or stroke shall pass from the Law until all is accomplished. Matthew 5:18 (NIV)

Prophecies on mental agony and physical ailments

He is despised and rejected of men; a man of sorrows, and acquainted with grief: and we hid as it were our faces from him; he was despised, and we esteemed him not. Surely he hath borne our grieves, and carried our sorrows: yet we did esteem him stricken, smitten of God, and afflicted.

But he was wounded for our transgressions; he was bruised for our iniquities: the chastisement of our peace was upon him; and with his stripes we are healed. Isa. 53:3-5

Here is one of the most profound prophecies of Isaiah concerning our mental, body and spiritual healing. God spoke through the prophecy of Isaiah that mental problems; grief, losses and all kinds of pain would be healed through the stripe of Jesus. Now when Jesus came he fulfilled his part of the prophecy by being subject to several gruesome body injuries in the hands of Roman Soldiers. What is next then?

What is next in the line of these prophecies is that all who are sick claim their healing. Think about it, if repentance of sin is prophesied and repenting brought about forgiveness of our sins, if other prophecies like the catching up of the saints or tribulation are considered valid and we expect their fulfillments in due time, we ought to expect our healing by reason of the death of Jesus Christ on the cross too.

Prophecies concerning blindness, deafness and paralysis

"Then the eyes of the blind shall be opened, and the ears of the deaf shall be unstopped. Then shall the lame man leap as an hart, and the tongue of the dumb sing: ...Isaiah 35:5-6

According to this prophecy, in the days of Jesus on earth (and in the days that follow of course) mighty creative miracles will take place. When Jesus came we saw this prophecies fulfilled. In the case of the man born blind whom Jesus healed, who the Pharisees also attempted to dissuade we hear saying that *Since the beginning of time it has never been heard that anyone opened the eyes of a person born blind* John 9:32 *(NASB)*

We see all these miracles through the ministry of Jesus. In fact it was upon this prophecy *Isa35:5-6* that Jesus established his messianic claim before John the Baptist. When John sent men to enquire if Jesus was the expected messiah he told them that the blind sees, the deaf hear. Today a blind person is not hopeless; if he believes in this prophecy he can have his blind eyes opened. This prophecy began with Jesus and is *'...for you and your children and for all who are far off— for all whom the Lord our God will call." Acts. 2:39*

The miracles God foretell through prophecy here are creative miracles. Blind eyes opening, deaf ears unstopped, lame men walking, and the dumb talking; these are all creative miracles. Anybody therefore missing body part through aging or auto accident can receive creative miracle through fulfillment of this prophecy in Isaiah. But just like any other prophecy one would have to pray, proclaim the prophecy and claim the prophecy for it to come to pass.

And the prophecy is always there for personal application just like forgiveness of sin. There are many people who have not accepted Jesus' forgiveness of sin. They are still in debate as to whether or not Jesus could indeed forgive sin. Until they come to the reality of this prophecy on forgiveness the burden of their sin is yet on them.

Prophecy on how problems will be destroyed

And it shall come to pass in that day, that his burden shall be taken away from off thy shoulder, and his yoke from off thy neck and the yoke shall be destroyed because of the anointing. Isaiah 10:27

Whenever you read the phrase 'in that day' it is referring to the new dispensation, the day in which we live; the new dispensation of grace through Jesus Christ our Lord. These are the days when through Jesus Christ every believer will receive the anointing. This anointing is the power of God in our lives. It makes it <u>impossible</u> for problems to 'stick' and if the problem is already there it corrodes the problem.

In Chapter five you will learn how to put these prophecies to work and receive your healing.

Prophecy on opening prison doors

*The Spirit of the Lord GOD is upon me, because the LORD has anointed me to bring good news to the afflicted; He has sent me to bind up the brokenhearted, to proclaim liberty to captives and freedom to prisoners; Isa. **61:1-2***

This is another prophecy of Isaiah concerning sickness, diseases and all the works of the devil. We know Jesus could not have been referring to local prison in the outskirt of your city. These prison must be Satan's erected building; Hell on earth; Invisible but real chamber of torture that men feel through physical ailment and deadly disease. Jesus sets us free from any of such prison. we can expect that prophecy fulfilled.

Prophecy on Laying hands to see recovery

*"These signs will accompany those who have believed: in My name they will cast out demons, they will speak with new tongues; they will pick up serpents, and if they drink any deadly poison, it will not hurt them; they will lay hands on the sick, and they will recover." Mark **16:18***

This may as well qualify as a prophecy since Jesus had not ascended at the time he spoke these words. We need to remember that Jesus operated as an Old Testament Prophet before His death. He said that if we as believers lay our hands on the sick the sick shall recover.

> *I submit to you that if a man hasn't discovered something that, he will die for, he isn't fit to live*
> Martin Luther King Jr.

CHAPTER 2

WHAT JESUS DID ABOUT YOUR ILLNESS

For we do not have a high priest who is unable to sympathize with our weaknesses. Instead, we have one who in every respect has been tempted as we are, yet he never sinned.   Hebrews 4:15 (International Standard Version)

I HAVE HEARD this rather silly argument from countless a good people. They would ask *'if Jesus really cares why is there so much evil in the world?'* And to this question, there is also this appropriate customary reply *'if there were so many laundry detergents in the world why do we still have dirty linen?* That really settles it. What is implied here is that Jesus is the detergent of the world. If one does not apply this detergent to cleanse oneself from the evil, the evil will remain. That is why despite the work of Jesus on the cross we have sicknesses everywhere.

Jesus is not only touched by our problems he did something about it. He died so that we may be redeemed from sickness. God is not only compassionate he is a proactive God. The *bible said, 'he gave his one and only Son, that whosoever believes in him shall not perish but have eternal life.* John 3:16 (NIV)

Sympathy or Substitution

Jesus did not come to merely sympathize and encourage us in our misery. The gospel of our Lord is more than encouragement and it is certainly not just a recipe for success. Jesus is not another Prophet who has come to warn us of impending danger. He is not a nationalist like Gandhi of India nor is he a human right figure like Martin Luther Jr, and Nelson Mandela to argue our cases before human government. Jesus is our substitution. He came to do something about our illness; He suffered in our place and through his *substitutionary* suffering and death, we are healed. Jesus is our substitution in two main ways.

The first part of the substitution: we are in Jesus

The way to understand Jesus substitution is to see his work as some kind of 'covert operation'. All the time he was suffering on that cross we were in him. So we were in the guise of Jesus. When he was being crucified and tortured, Jesus felt the pain but it was our sickness and diseases in our body of sin that was being put to death. When the devil looks at us he does not see us, he sees Jesus being put to death. Take a look at the following scriptures.

He made Him who knew no sin to be sin on our behalf, 2 Cor. 5:21a
In whom (Jesus) also ye are circumcised with the circumcision made without hands, in putting off the body of the sins of the flesh by the circumcision of Christ: Col. 2:11
The word of God *says also, that 'He was wounded for our transgressions, He was bruised for our iniquities; the chastisement for our peace was upon Him, and by His stripes we are healed.' Isa 53:5*

As he took the stripes, the body of our sin, that is, our old nature with the disease and sickness residing in it was destroyed. That is the first part of the substitution.

The second part of substitution: Jesus is in us

The second substitution took place at the Resurrection of Jesus. When he rose from the grave, the situation was reversed. In the second part of the substitution Jesus disguised as the believer; that is, Jesus is now in us. Jesus is in us commanding and torturing devils. Though the world sees us, the works we do is not really us that does it but Jesus that is in us. <u>Remember in the first part we were in Jesus; he carried us in him and bore the suffering from the devil on the cross. In the second part; he is in us torturing the devil through us.</u>

There is a scripture that summarizes both the first and second substitution:

I am <u>crucified with Christ</u>: **(first operation)** *nevertheless I live; yet not I, but <u>Christ liveth in me</u>:* **(second operation)** *and the life which I now live in the flesh I live by the faith of the Son of God, who loved me, and gave himself for me. Gal. 2:20* (words in parenthesis added).

Also again here we see that Christ is in us now doing amazing things through our body.
To whom God would make known what is the riches of the glory of this mystery among the Gentiles; which is <u>Christ in you,</u> the hope of glory: Col. 1:27

When he atoned for your sins, he healed you

To atone means *to make amends for, to make reparation for, to make restitution for, to make up for, to compensate for, or to pay for.* Jesus did just that for us.

The prophet Isaiah prophesied very clearly the accomplishment of Jesus on the cross in the book of Isaiah. It says Jesus has borne our grieves and carried our sorrows. That means he has paid for our sins. In doing this he procured our healing.

'Surely he hath **borne** *our grieves, and* **carried** *our sorrows: yet we did esteem him stricken, smitten of God, and afflicted. But he was wounded for our transgressions; he was bruised for our iniquities: the chastisement of our peace was upon him; and with his stripes we are healed.' Isa. 53: 4-6*

Surely...[Jesus] Bore our Grieves
[Jesus] Carried our sorrows
[Jesus] Wounded for our transgression

[Jesus] Bruised for our iniquities
[Jesus] Chastised for our peace

We were Healed by [Jesus] stripes

People fret about the willingness of God to heal. They say something like *'is it the will of God to heal me? Am I too old for healing? Am I too far-gone in sin that God is unwilling to heal me?* The Good news is that He healed us ever before therefore rendering those questions unnecessary. He healed you though He knew you were going to make mistake.

The Scripture above says *'He hath borne our Grieves'* borne is a past participle stating what has already being done at the time in question. God is not planning to heal nor is He thinking to heal anyone. He already healed everyone including you when He sent his son to the cross. Also the scripture says He carried our sorrows. Carried is in past tense, which again means that this mission of carrying our sorrows has already being accomplished. Glory be to God! We need not worry that we might not be on the healing list. We all are!

'By his Stripes we are healed' is letting us know evidently that we have been healed. *'Healed'* again is in the past. This shows that once healed, we remain or stay healed.

Your sickness is part of what he carried away

The text we read above saying 'He bore our grieves and carried our sorrows' can be properly rendered as he bore our sicknesses and carried our Pain...

The Hebraic Roots Bible reads;

Surely he has borne our sicknesses, and he carried our pain...and with his wound we were healed...Isa 53:4-6 (Hebraic Roots Bible)

This is because the Hebrew Word translated into English as grief is *cholly [pronounced* khol·ē' *]* This word actually mean sickness. Cholly mean sickness. And the Hebrew word translated as sorrows is the word makob [pronounced mak·ōve'] It can also be translated as pain; physical pain and mental pain. A better rendition would therefore read 'surely he hath borne our sicknesses and He carried both our physical and mental pain'. The word translated bore is the Hebrew word 'nasa' which means *'carry away; take away, bear.*

Thus the scripture says *Jesus carried away our sickness....'*

If something were carried away, that thing is no longer where it used to be. It is gone! It is now somebody else's problem. Jesus made your problem his problem. So JESUS did not only atone for your sins by his death, he took off your sickness first by his suffering. *'By his stripes we are healed.'* A stripe is a bruise or wound trickling down with blood. By these stripes we have been healed. The apostle of Jesus Christ; Apostle Peter declared this truth also in the book of Peter.

Who his own self bare our sins in his own body on the tree, that we, being dead to sins, should live unto righteousness: by whose stripes ye were healed 1 Pet 2:24

The Little girl and the Bible

A man once told a story of a little girl who was given up to die by Doctors. The girl reading the bible came across this passage where the scripture says, *he bore our sins in his own body.* ¹ᴾᵉᵗᵉʳ ²:²⁴ She became excited and said with a smile of relief on her face *'mommy, I can now die and go to heaven because Jesus forgave me of my sins.'* She then read further and found where it says *'by whose stripes ye were healed'.* This little girl became even more excited. She happily and confidently announced to her mother that she was not going to die after all. -- That Jesus has healed her. That was it for her! She began to get well from that moment.

People would always ask; if this is true what do I do to receive my healing? Just believe this with your heart and proclaim it as a fact and you will soon realize you are well. Start doing what you can't do. Declare that you are healed no matter how you feel. Your feeling may lie to you but your body will eventually conform to God's word.

The truth is that if you are saved you are already healed. That is, if you have received Jesus as your savior and you are absolutely convinced that Jesus took away your sins, then you are already healed too. What Jesus did on Calvary is not a partial work. It is an all-inclusive work. We sometimes erroneously present the work of Jesus in fragments as though He forgives our sins first, and a little later, He cleanses us from sin and maybe if we get lucky, He then heal our diseases. Calvary is not only about forgiveness. It is about deliverance from sin, sickness and poverty. It is by faith that we accept the forgiveness of our sins and only by faith can we realize our healing too.

We may not have felt forgiven at first, but we believed that our sins are forgiven. It is after we have accepted the forgiveness of our sins by faith that we begin to feel the assurance of forgiveness in our soul. We feel the burden lifted off and heavenly Joy flood our soul. It is the same with healing. We must first accept it, to experience the reality in our lives. For a lot of people to accept something they cannot feel or see is difficult. As you read this book I pray the Holy Ghost help you to be able to believe what God says even when you have not felt it. Jesus says blessed are those who believe without seeing.

Jesus saith unto him, Thomas, because thou hast seen me, thou hast believed: blessed [are] they that have not seen, and [yet] have believed. John 20:29

When a person refuses to believe that Jesus has healed him or her, this person may never experience the healing Jesus procured for him or her.

Jesus Just like Moses

The ministry of Jesus Christ has been compared to that of Moses. If you understand the Ministry of Moses, you will understand the Ministry of Jesus. Referring to Jesus, Moses prophesied that *God will raise up for you a Prophet like me (Moses)* $^{Deut\ 18:12}$
The ministry of Moses was a shadow of Jesus' Ministry. As Moses dealt Egypt devastating blow by doing signs and wonders in there, so did Jesus in the street of Palestine. Moses did not go to Egypt to organize a rally or protest. He did not negotiate with Pharaoh; In fact, he gave Pharaoh an ultimatum to let Israel go. He turned the nation of Egypt upside-down and left Egypt broken in several places. So did Jesus in the days preceding his passion on the cross. He went about healing, and casting out devils; Hell was in commotion and demons were on flight.

This was to fulfill what was spoken through the prophet Isaiah: "He took up our infirmities and bore our diseases." Matt. 8:17

Jesus took away people's diseases and delivered them from the oppression of the devil. **Jesus surmised that sickness is of the devil:**

And he was teaching in one of the synagogues on the Sabbath. And, behold, there was a woman which had a spirit of infirmity eighteen years, and was bowed together, and could in no wise lift up herself. Luke 13:10-11

Jesus attributed her condition to demonic works and said:

'...ought not this woman, being a daughter of Abraham, whom Satan hath bound, lo, these eighteen years, be loosed from this bond on the Sabbath day?' Luke 13:16

The devil thought he would get rid of Jesus but Jesus did the unthinkable!

Even in the grave Jesus is Lord

He went to the cross. It was his ticket to hell where he would completely disarm the enemy. Imagine! Of what benefit is it to be healed if after Jesus departure the devil afflicts them again? And how do we who live now benefit from Jesus when he has departed the earth? Jesus had to take from the devil the power to afflict. That is why he went down to hell (or the grave) as some would love to call it. I would not want to get into theological debate at this time as to where Jesus was exactly; Grave, Hell or Sheol. It is enough to know he went to the headquarters of devils.

With demons still reeling from the blows they suffered from Jesus because of all the countless miracles Jesus did, Jesus went on to hell to wreak even more irreparable and irreversible havoc. Just like that night, Under Moses' watch when God killed the firstborn of every household in Egypt and Egypt was very sore, Jesus also went to hell, the headquarters of devils to kill and pulverize too.

Jesus *"descended first into the lower parts of the earth?" Eph 4:9;* **down** the abyss, where he threw off principalities and disarmed powers.

The bible said, and having spoiled principalities and powers, he made a shew of them openly, triumphing over them in it. Col 2:15

This is the climax of the work of Christ. He emerged from the grave declaring ultimate victory;

I am the Living One; I was dead, and now look, I am alive forever and ever! And I hold the keys of death and Hades. Rev. 1:18 (NIV)

When Jesus went to the cross he took our sickness with him. When he died our sickness and diseases died with him too. And when he rose up we rose up with him afresh- a new person. There is no place for sickness and disease anymore.

We were buried therefore with him by baptism into death, in order that, just as Christ was raised from the dead by the glory of the Father, we too might walk in newness of life. Rom 6:4

The saying is trustworthy, for: If we have died with him, we will also live with him; 2 Tim. 2:11-13

No matter how serious your illness may be, it does not matter if medical science has not found any cure- the demon responsible for that sickness had been defeated forever. There is hope for you if you believe these things.

If you are saved you are healed

This inadmissible fragmentation of the work of Jesus Christ has been going on for a while; A situation where after we have received Christ and have acknowledge the forgiveness of our sins we await yet for a subsequent work of grace expecting God to do something else about our sickness. We are saying in essence that we do not believe that when we got saved we got healed too. That is, we believe God is more willing to save us from sin than from sickness. With sickness we think he has a different set of rules.

The result is that we have a lot of believers who are sick waiting for another salvation from sickness and demons. The word Salvation occurs over one hundred and sixty four times in the Bible. In both the New Testament and Old Testament it mean the same thing.

In Hebrew it is *Yasa* and it occur in so many scripture such as :

*"Surely Behold God is my **salvation**; I will trust and not be afraid.*
*The Lord, the Lord Jehovah, is my strength and my song; he has become my **salvation**.*
*Therefore with joy shall you draw water out of the wells of **salvation**." Isaiah 12:2-3*

Yasa translated to salvation means *width, spaciousness, freedom from constraint.* It also means *deliverance, salvation, rescue, safety, and welfare.* It is clear that salvation portrays freedom from sickness among so many others.

In the New Testament the word soteria is translated '*salvation*' For example in the Scriptures:

For I am not ashamed of the gospel of Christ: for it is the power of God unto **salvation** *(soteria) to everyone that believeth; to the Jew first, and also to the Greek. Rom. 1:16* (others Acts 7:25; 27:31; Hebrews 11:7 etc.).

'*Soteria*' is a noun translated '**salvation**' *and sozo is the verb meaning 'to* **save**'

In places where it is not translated '**salvation**' it is translated wholeness. When Jesus healed people he sometimes tells them that they were made whole. The word translated whole is the same word translated salvation or soundness and health. Also it means rescue, deliverance and cure. We therefore see that salvation is not forgiveness of sin only. Salvation in the New Testament definitely connotes health; being saved from:

1. Disease (Matthew 9:22; James 5:15 Mark 5:34)
2. Physical affliction (Hebrews 11:7)
3. Demon possession (Matthew 15:22; Mark 7:26, 29)
4. Death (Hebrews 5:7; Acts 27:20, 31)
5. Spiritual threats (Romans 8:38, 39)
6. Sin (Romans 5:9; Hebrews 7:25)

It is evident that the work of salvation is a complete work including deliverance from sickness. If we are not fully informed we cannot be fully blessed either.

Our faith is from level to level and from dimension to dimension. When we become saved, we have a measure of faith and we continue to go higher ever after. We do not need to start seeking for salvation from sickness again.

Sin and sickness same and alike

Sin is frowned upon but sickness is tolerated. We are usually ashamed of sin but sentimental about sickness. A man would usually call for prayer in order to be free from sickness even in an open meeting but the same would be too ashamed to let a Pastor into episodes of his struggle with sin. This is because there is this traditional belief that sin is from the devil but sickness is a normal part of life; that sin is an embarrassing admission of defeat but sickness is understandably beyond our control. Some even believe that sickness could come from God for a particular purpose. Undergirded by this notion they would not hesitate to pray for a sinner but for a sick person they must first find out if it is God's will.

In God's view however, every sickness and sin are same and alike. They are both the works of the devil. When Jesus went to the cross, he did not die for our sins only, he died to take away our sickness too. He was no more tolerant of sickness than he was of sin. There are no separate work for sin and for sickness. Healing is in the atonement.

When a person gets born again sin is as far removed from him as the east is from the west- Likewise, sickness and disease. These things become an external force attempting to destroy the believer. Sickness and sin becomes an external enemy. You are now in union with God against sin and sickness.

*Faith does not ignore the facts,
it ignores the power of the facts. --Benny Hinn*

CHAPTER 3

DISOLVING DOUBTS

THE DEVIL DID not appear to Jesus bodily in those forty days of his temptation. The devil registered his presence through thoughts and imagination. If this were not the case, somebody else would have spotted the devil considering the temptation spanned a period of forty days in three noticeable locations; the wilderness, the mountain and the temple. The devil tempted Jesus exactly the same way we all are tempted. We usually don't see the devil in boxing gloves with our optical eyes. He comes through our minds bringing in doubt. Jesus was tempted through a barrage of negative, demeaning thoughts. The devil started by casting doubt on Jesus son-ship, *'If you are the Son of God,* tell these stones to become loaves of bread' [Mat. 4:3]

Doubt is the anonymous presence of the devil, the effect of which we feel through array of negative demonic thoughts. I used to think that doubt is merely negative information that easily can be erased. Far from it, rather it is the work of masquerading evil spirits. The most ferocious attack of the devil takes place in the mind and it is preceded by flood of doubts. Sicknesses are welcomed to stay when people entertain demonic thoughts in their mind. Sicknesses are also sustained by enduring these negative, hopeless thoughts. Since these thoughts are not just straying thought but the devil's unseen presence, only a true encounter with Jesus can cure a person of doubt. Doubt is the only thing that stands between us and the blessing of healing through Jesus. In this chapter God will dissolve the power of doubt even further by aiming gospel light at some of the fondest thoughts in the mind of the sick.

Am I in good standing that God is willing to heal me?

You may be fighting one of the most popular demonic antics; that tiny taunting voice, *'am I in good reputation before God that He would be willing to heal me?'* I have seen people do charitable works in the hope of earning healing from God. They think these works afford them a good image before Him. We are all prone to think that way at some point in our faith journey, especially when we consider the utmost greatness of God. And for those intending to please Him or receive from Him, the sense of His awesome greatness places a responsibility far too overwhelming on them. We are aware of God's power, and the fact that we ought to go to Him for help, but we are not sufficiently aware of His enormous love that we actually go to Him. I mean we know about the power of God, but we are often unaware of His unfathomable love. Understanding God's love is more important than understanding His power. Most people believe in the power of God, but the challenge many people face is the difficulty in believing in God's personal love for them.

He loves us so much that He is willing to give His son and if *'He that spared not his own Son, but delivered him up for us all, how shall he not with him also freely give us all things?' Rom 8:32*
Jesus never denied anyone healing on the account of their imperfections nor on the basis of their status in the society. Jesus loves us *'even while we are yet sinners'* Rom 5:8

God commendeth his love toward us, in that, while we were yet sinners, Christ died for us. Rom 5:8

If he died for us while we were yet sinners why will he not heal us when we are now believers? He surely will. Besides it is not by works that we are healed. It is by faith. It is this faith in the love of God that cleanses us; it propels us to Him and that give us access to divine healing. If we keep looking at our works we will never be holy enough in our own eyes. We will keep allowing the accusative voice to debar us from going *'boldly to the throne of grace'* Heb 4:16

It is with regard to this that Apostle Paul declared *'Therefore it is of faith that it might be according to grace, so that the promise might be sure to all the seed, not only to those who are of the law, but also to those who are of the faith of Abraham, who is the father of us all...Romans 4:16*
Please, pay utmost attention to the phrase '<u>so that the promise might be sure to all</u>'. It says God made sure our healing is by faith and not by works so that it will be

sure to come to everyone who believes. This tells us that healing is not by works, that is, not by self-effort of righteousness, or personal holiness, if that were not the case, some people would never qualify to receive healing. So it is not by merit whatsoever. Whosoever believes that Jesus Christ died on the cross and took away his or her sickness and diseases is not only saved, but healed as well.

I know a man who tried to believe God for a child because his wife could not conceive. He later told me God wanted him to build a school and that if he obeys and build, the children he so wanted would come. I knew better but I could not convince him otherwise. He built the school. Five years after the fact he and his wife were still without children. Then he said if he resigned from his job and work in a charitable organization his wife would conceive. He resigned and another five years passed without any child in sight. This man was imposing conditions for his own healing; Imaginary conditions that God never require of him when he could just trust in God's love.

We must be careful not to 'mortgage' our healing by imposing sanction on ourselves.

Jesus Christ already paid what is required to obtain healing on our behalf. The question of whether God will or will not heal should never arise. It was paid for long ago and it was for everybody; sinner and saint.

Can my past sin hinder me from being healed?

You may be thinking you have committed the unpardonable sin - something so grave that God decide not heal you. Perhaps you say 'God warned me again and again but I failed to heed the warnings therefore God's patience has run out on me.'

As I stated earlier, healing has already been paid for, the question of whether God is willing to heal you or not should not arise. Faith for healing is not an attempt to convince God to heal it is the laying hold of the healing God already provided. You will notice that after the resurrection of Christ prayer takes a new dimension. Prayer used to be merely asking and receiving. Now a higher dimension of prayer, which is accessing and receiving, is possible, Jesus having obtained for us eternal inheritance. Jesus Christ has made everything available to us.

Prayer is now the act of *taking it and holding on to it.* It is no longer an arduous effort to convince God to give us anything. God has given us all things. Even as the great Apostle also make us to know:

He that spared not his own Son, but delivered him up for us all, how shall he not with him also freely give us all things? Romans 8:32.

You will also see promises like *'...According as his divine power hath given unto us all things that pertain unto life and godliness...' 2 Pet 1:3*

And again in the book of Ephesians *'...Father of our Lord Jesus Christ, who hath blessed us with all spiritual blessings in heavenly places in Christ:'*
Eph 1:3

The common thread in these scriptures is that you have been given all things.
Since '...*All things are yours;*' 1 Cor. 3:21b all you need to do is receive what has been given to you and hold on to it.

'Lambano' it

That is the reason you see that in many passages in the bible, after the death and resurrection of Christ we are urged to receive what we need rather than ask.

> *Receive the Holy Spirit' Acts 2:38,*
> *Receive remission of sins. Acts 10:43*
> *Receive abundance of grace and of the gift of righteousness Romans 5:17*
> *Receive the promise of the Spirit through faith. Gal 3:14*

The word translated *'receive'* is the Greek word 'Lambano' it means *catch it and hold on to it.* Much the same way a football player would catch a ball and fight off an opponent to hold onto the ball.
Since *Lambano* mean *catch it and hold onto it.* Do not stand wondering if God wants to heal you. Catch the healing that is thrown to you and hold onto it. In Chapter five I will discuss how you can take hold of that *for which Christ Jesus took hold of for you* $^{Phil\ 3:12}$

What are the sins that can hinder me from being healed?

The only sin that can hinder a person's healing is doubt. I use the word sin because anything done without faith is sin. Sin can only bring back the sickness after you have been healed. No other sin except doubt can stop your healing. Because when Jesus comes to you he takes away both the sin and sickness. He does not decline healing you because of your sin(s). The bible says;

He has not dealt with us according to our sins, nor rewarded us according to our iniquities. Psalm 103:10

Your sin can only affect you if you go back to it after you have been healed, in which case a worse condition may develop. Just like it was in the case of the man born Jesus healed who was born blind. Jesus healed him and did not bring up the issue of his past sin but later warned him that if he went back to sin a worse condition might develop.

Afterward Jesus found him in the temple and said unto him, "Behold, thou art made whole. Sin no more, lest a worse thing come unto thee." John 5:14 (NIV)

This is not a tacit encouragement to sin. Sin can interfere with your ability to believe God, in which case it can hinder your healing indirectly. But the idea is that I don't want you to allow the accusing voice of the devil slamming you with allegations of imperfection and advancing that as a basis of your unworthiness for healing. If we wait until we are error-free we would never be healed. We believe in Christ *'that we might be justified by the faith of Christ and not by works, for by the works of the law shall no man be justified.*
Gal 2:16b&c

Jesus Healed all

Consider all the multitude of people Jesus healed, could they all have been perfect?

But Jesus, aware of this, withdrew from there. Many followed Him, and He healed them all... Matthew 12:15

Jesus will heal you regardless of your moral estate if only you can believe on him. Not only will he take away the sickness, he will also take away the sin associated with it because *'he is faithful and just to forgive us our sins and to cleanse us from all wickedness...1 John 1:9*

This sickness runs in my family

When a Child is born, we could say a father is born too. Likewise, when you become born-again, you also have a new Father - our Father who is in heaven. ^{Matt 6:9-13}

Yet to all who did receive him, to those who believed in his name, he gave the right to become children of God— children born not of natural descent, nor of human decision or a husband's will, but born of God. John 1:12-13 (NIV)

It is very clear that the writer is not talking figuratively. You may be wondering *'but is everybody not a child of God?'* The answer is no—everybody is not a child of God as the scripture above clearly suggest. We are all creatures of God but we are not all children of God. Only those who have been born again are the children of God. And if you don't like the expression, born again, that is okay, we can say those who have truly become a believer in the Lord Jesus Christ, those who truly believe that he died and God raised him up, are considered Children of God. Jesus himself talked about this new family when he declined to see his mother.

Who is my mother? and who are my brethren?
And he stretched forth his hand toward his disciples, and said, Behold my mother and my brethren!

For whosoever shall do the will of my Father which is in heaven, the same is my brother, and sister, and mother. Matt 12:46-50

What I want us to see is that in this new family, there is no sickness and disease or genetic disorder. To suggest otherwise is to suggest that God almighty is susceptible to disease. So, to which family do you belong?

What about Job of old?

Everybody knows the story of Job; God supposedly allowed Satan to hurt him even while God consider him righteous. What a contradiction! If we are not careful two things will happen after reading the story of Job; first, we may justify the condition we are going through as consistent with that of Job. Second, we may think God is unjust and develop at least a subtle aversion toward God. In both cases we are hurting ourselves. Yet the word of God is meant to bless us not hurt us. The popular interpretation of Job's suffering has hurt us more than blessed us. People who believe that God would make Satan hurt Job just to prove a point are not willing that God do the same thing to them. It is obvious something is not right.

The trial of Job has been misconstrued as permission issued by God to Satan to attack faithful Job for experimental purposes. Many therefore, who suffering for a long time has justified their illness as another case of Job. The enemy often takes a perfect scripture meant for our blessing and whips us with it. And this is the case with Job.

First, it is inconsistent with God's nature to bring sickness upon people, let alone supposedly a God-fearing person like Job. Second, what kind of God will enter into A BET with the health of His Children?

So what really happened that day when Job's case came up?

And the LORD said unto Satan, Hast thou considered my servant Job, that there is none like him in the earth, a perfect and an upright man, one that feareth God, and escheweth evil?

Then Satan answered the LORD, and said, doth Job fear God for naught?
Hast not thou made an hedge about him, and about his house, and about all that he hath on every side? Thou hast blessed the work of his hands, and his substance is increased in the land.
But put forth thine hand now, and touch all that he hath, and he will curse thee to thy face.

And the LORD said unto Satan, Behold, all that he hath is in thy power; only upon himself put not forth thine hand. So Satan went forth from the presence of the LORD.

Yes! God bragged about Job as he would love to brag about all His children before a devil who goes about accusing them. But that is all He did. At the time however, without God's doing, the situation was already ripe for Job's trial. How?

Though Job was no doubt a good man of morally impeccable standard, but *Job was living in fear in certain areas of his life.* We usually do not notice this because we focus on sin of omission and sin of commission—*the dos and don'ts,* but there is a whole new class of sin which does not fascinate us and certainly may not come under the radar of the puritans but are nonetheless dangerous. These are sins of disposition like doubt, fear, and evil imagination e.t.c. this was the weakness and undoing of Job. Here is Job's own confession when he became ill.

*For the thing which I greatly **feared** is come upon me, and that which I was **afraid** of is come unto me. I was **not in safety**, neither had I rest, neither was I quiet; yet trouble came. Job 3:24, 25*

He said negative things that, if today we say the same thing we would as soon generate problem of proportionate magnitude. He said *'I feared'*, *'I was afraid'*, *'I was not in safety'*, *'I did not have rest'*, and he said *'I was not quiet,'*

Now it is easy to see that by these negative confessions Job in the days before his trial, had heaved himself into the hand of Satan. He was ripe for trial. Nobody talks like Job and remain protected. The hedge is broken, the serpent shall bite. All God told Satan is well, I know he is already in your hand only don't take his life. Watch it! He was reading Satan Job's rights.

*And the LORD said unto Satan, **Behold, all that he hath is in thy power;** only upon himself put not forth thine hand. So Satan went forth from the presence of the LORD. Job 1:12 (emphasis added)*

'Behold' does not mean I give you permission. *'Behold'* mean, *'see'*, *Look*, it is pointing you to *what* already *is*. Not *what is about to be*. Job was already in Satan's hand but Satan still had to take permission from God; he had to know what Job's right are under the circumstances.

Today, God can't have such conversation with the devil because the accuser of our brethren is not only *'cast down'*, he is also been *'cast out'*. [Rev 12:9,10]

Job inadvertently invited trouble. This is true because it is much more difficult to believe that God would permit Satan to strike an innocent man.

Was Job all the better for the sickness?

We never read of Job learning anything new in his ordeal. If anybody learnt anything it is the devil. He learnt except of course other than his fear that Job was truly faithful to God. He learnt that God is right. Sickness can only teach us what we refuse to learn when we are in health. Nobody whips an innocent student in order to teach him lesson. Whiplashes are for those who won't learn. God may teach us things when we are sick but He does not need sickness to teach us anything. God teaches us with His Word all the time taking advantage of circumstances in our lives.

All scripture is given by inspiration of God, and is profitable for doctrine, for reproof, for correction, for instruction in righteousness: 2 Tim 3:16

Sickness and diseases are not correctional tools. People who come out of sickness a better person are those that survive the post sickness syndrome. Usually sickness makes people bitter and weaker in faith. If sickness produced faith then sick people in the hospitals should have more faith than people who are not sick. But we know this is not true. It is the word of God alone that produce faith.

...So then faith cometh by hearing, and hearing by the word of God. Romans 10:17

Am already old –this sickness could Be from God

A wonderful brother asked me if there was any use in praying for his friend. I asked what he meant and he replied 'he is already old and I think this might as well be the sickness that will take him home'

I told him he could pray for anybody because Jesus paid for the sickness of old men and women too. The bible did not suggest that *'By his stripe we are healed (with the exception of old people)* [1 Pet 2:24]

Paul Prayed for Publius father who could well have been an old man.

And it came to pass, that the father of Publius lay sick of a fever and of a bloody flux: to whom Paul entered in, and prayed, and laid his hands on him, and healed him. Acts 28:7-8

There is no way to tell the age of Publius father, but most likely, he must have been an old man. Publius was the chief of the Island. He could not have been a young man to have held such an elderly position as chief man of the Island.

Healed at eighty

An 80-year old lady came to me for prayer. She was dying of cancer. She taught it was time for her to die. The first thing I told her? "Ma'am you are going to live! God is going to heal your cancer and you decide how you want to go to heaven when you are ready." I told her I don't want her thinking in her mind that this sickness was from God and was meant to take her home. Glory be to God, she believed with me and got healed her of the cancer. She is still going as strong today as anyone can be.

If I keep getting healed how am I ever going to die?

There are people who have passed into heaven without seeing death. They took their breath with them to heaven. And though they are still going to have to lay that life down at some point but they showed us that death is not the only way to go to heaven. One of them is Enoch.

By faith Enoch was translated that he should not see death; and was not found, because God had translated him: for before his translation he had this testimony, that he pleased God. Hebrews 11:5

The same word used for Enoch — *translated,* is used for the believer in Christ too.
(God) Who hath delivered us from the power of darkness, and hath **translated** *us into the kingdom of his dear Son: Col 1:13 (word in bracket added)*

If Enoch was translated that he could not see death. The believer in Christ is translated too. We who believe in Christ should not have to be sick before we go on to heaven. We also can lay down our lives willingly and depart without sickness. Another person that did not see death is Prophet Elijah:

...And Elijah went up to heaven in a whirlwind. 2 King 2:11

He went up to heaven in a whirlwind. Not by cancer, heart failure or any of those diseases but in a whirlwind.

Worrying about how we are going to go to heaven should not be our preoccupation.

Old age sickness is not of God

People talk about *aging-associated diseases* as though it is something we must all expect. To grow mature is of God. To grow with aging-associated diseases such as Cancer, Arthritis, Dementia, Cataract, Osteoporosis, diabetes, hypertension and Alzheimer's is not from God. It is not the way God designed our lives.

Just like I said you don't have to '*die*' in order to go to heaven – you can just lay your life down or even hold on to it and later submit it. The same can be said of aging. Old age does not have to come with weakness and development of certain diseases such as high blood pressure, hypertension etc... You can advance in years yet remain strong and beautiful.

Wrinkles and rickety bones are not signs of advanced years they are sign of worry and *aging, both of* which are satanic operations. Aging is a chemical process set in motion by demonic spirit to stop our bodies from renewal. Again scripture is clear that '*aging*' is not of God. *God satisfies your mouth with good things, so that your youth is renewed like the eagle.*^{Psalm 103:5} Whenever people walk in a superior light such as the gospel they can defy that deadly chemical process set in motion by demonic spirits. Caleb defied aging. Caleb is one of the two original Israelites left that made the promise land according to the word of God. Caleb was eighty-five years old when he took the mountain. Imagine how strong he could have been to go to war. At eighty-five years of age making a case for himself to go to war he said;

..and now, lo, I am this day eighty-five years old. As yet I am as strong this day as I was in the day that Moses sent me: as my strength was then, even so is my strength now, for war, both to go out, and to come in. Joshua 14:10

He declared that in the past forty years his physical strength had remained intact. Amazing! I know scientifically, this is nonsense. Many a times the word of God doesn't make sense but it works. Again, the case of Moses is yet another scenario of <u>age defiance</u>:

And Moses was an hundred and twenty years old when he died: his eye was not dim, nor his natural force abated. **Deut 34:7**

Moses had to be told to go and die. He lay down and decided to die. It was like he lay down and called death to come. Interesting! At one hundred and twenty years, he did not decline in health. He had no symptoms such as dimming vision, sclerosis, and muscle loss.

Even in the days preceding the Law People lived to be Nine hundred years (900 years) and above in this same body. They did not have a superior genetic make-up. Symptoms of old age could not set in until they were well over 800 years old. Adam lived 930 years, Jared lived 962 years and Methuselah who lived the longest lived to be 969 years. Yet upon them was the curse of death. How long should we expect of the believer from whom all curses have been lifted and upon whom the grace of God has come?

Time will fail me to write about Sarah the wife of Abraham who at sixty -five years was found irresistible by men. Sarah's beauty earned her another name – Yiskah ("Jessica"), meaning "Seer," 'because people used to gaze at her beauty' (Talmud, Megillah 14a). Even at old age 'Sarah was exceptionally beautiful, and all other women, by comparison with her, looked like monkeys (Talmud, Bava Batra 58a).

All these wonderful saints have the same body like ours yet they defied aging. Aging is part of the curse. It is a consequence of the misfortune in Eden. Since that time, there is a spirit that fight the regeneration of our cells. Even doctors cannot explain why we die because the body is made to renew itself. The truth is that it is a demonic spirit that is responsible for this. And once we are sufficiently acquainted with the power of God to renew our youth like the eagles, we soon find we can defy aging too.

How do I know I am healed when I don't feel healed?

It's possible that you are healed yet symptoms of sickness remain. How is that? Healing occurs first in the spirit at which point the body may not have received signal of healing. Therefore you may know you are healed by divine knowledge coming from your spirit yet with all the symptoms of the illness still present in your body. The knowledge of your healing is of the spirit; a divine knowledge if you will, it is a spiritual revelation impacted into your human spirit.

When Jesus prayed for the ten lepers, there was no instant physical healing. All symptoms of leprosy were still fully present. I believe they knew something has happened in their lives otherwise they would not have left Jesus alone. It was as they went on their way, time passing that they experienced the physical reality of their healing.

As He entered a village, 10 men with serious skin diseases met Him. They stood at a distance and raised their voices, saying, "Jesus, Master, have mercy on us!" When He saw them, He told them, "Go and show yourselves to the priests." And while they were going, they were healed. Luke 17:14 (Holman Christian Standard Bible)

Divine healing occurs in the human spirit, at which point one may not have any feeling in the physical body. Then the spirit sends information to the body. It is at this point that one begins to see the results in the body. If this process happens so quickly that it is impossible to tell that a communication between the spirit and the body took place we say that the miracle is instantaneous. If one however lost faith because there is no apparent physical change then one may have destroyed the chances that any healing in the physical body occur. Feeling always follows faith, and faith is the divine knowledge of our healing. It is never the reverse. Jesus put it this way;

Jesus saith unto him, Thomas, because thou hast seen me, thou hast believed: blessed are they that have not seen, and yet have believed. John 20:29

I know I am healed because I know God's word is true. The ability to believe and see what is not visible to others is faith. It is also a blessing from God. That is why Jesus said those who express such remarkable divine ability to know what is not obvious to others are blessed.

The woman who defied the symptoms Of leukemia

There was this woman who left the United States to Nigeria for prayer. She was very convinced of her healing after prayer. When she got back to the States she told her Doctor that she has been healed. The Doctor did a test on the woman, but contrary to her expectation her blood count had doubled. That is, the illness has worsened since the last time. But this woman was still thoroughly convinced that she has been healed though the Doctor told her that the cancer cells had increased in her blood.

She did the next ridiculous thing; she attempted to get pregnant. She had been warned by her Doctor prior to this time not to attempt to get pregnant because of her illness. She was told the illness would prevent pregnancy and that even if she did ever get pregnant she wouldn't be able to carry the baby to term. Despite the Doctor's warning she tried to get pregnant. First she went around parading herself as pregnant and asking people to congratulate her on her imaginary pregnancy. It was not long before her Doctor, the same doctor that had told her that her blood count had doubled confirmed that she was indeed pregnant and warned her again of the risk and advised her to terminate the pregnancy for fear of her very life. Contrariwise, and to the glory of God, defying all science the lady delivered the baby safely. What a miracle!

Finally, the greatest miracle of all happened; she tested negative to cancer after her delivery. God is good! Think about it, although the symptoms were present after the prayer, she was absolutely convinced she had been healed, and she received what she believed. Right after the prayer in Nigeria, the woman received a divine knowledge of her healing, when her body was yet to

reflect it. it was on this divine knowledge of her healing she stood.
I pray that faith is impacted into you now in Jesus name. Amen!

> *We will get to doctrinal differences once
> we have exhausted the riches of Jesus Christ.
> (Frank Viola, "Essential Ingredients")*

CHAPTER 4

FAR-REACHING IMPLICATIONS OF THE GOSPEL OF OUR LORD

CHRISTIANITY HAS A science. No religion does. Christianity has a science in the sense that it can be tested and proven. Mere religion cannot be proven. Only people are nudged or even coarse to embrace blind dogma and creeds to no end. If Jesus were alive today as we so claim then Jesus can do the same miracles he did yesterday, today and forever. This is one of the far-reaching implications of the gospel of our Lord. Religion tells people to hope. Christianity makes hope a reality. For those of us who believe, here are some of the mighty implications of our faith with regard to healing and health.

Do Christians die? Or they lay their lives down

To die means, to be killed, or for the life of a person to expire. For many death is a penalty; a violent involuntary end of life. For the one who is indeed a christian this can never happen. As long as God lives in a person it is impossible for the cell in his or her body to die. Death does not happen to a Christian if he lives the Christian life. The Christian does not die but only lay down his life as he chooses. This is because Jesus not only conquered sickness he conquered death! We do not have to remain afraid of death any longer. Our new birth in Christ has given us new life - the life of God. The very kind of life God has. God does not die. Jesus Christ lives forever! God has a life that is different from human life. That life is the life we receive. Jesus said God has granted him authority that *'he might give eternal life to those God have given him.' John 17:2*

And because Jesus lives we (believers) 'also will live' 'He that believes in me (Jesus) shall never die... John 14:19, John 11:25

Every Christian that is born again enjoys immunity from the power of death. That is what the Scripture is saying. As long as Jesus is alive we also will be alive. If we are ready to go to heaven we could lay down our life just like Jesus laid down his life willingly. When Pilate boasted of being able to save Jesus from death; Jesus answered him that He (Jesus) was not at anyone's mercy.

Jesus answered, Thou couldest have no power at all against me, except it were given thee from above: therefore he that delivered me unto thee hath the greater sin. John 19:11

Jesus said of his life that it was his choice to lay it down for us. Nobody or nothing could have killed him.

*"For this reason the Father loves Me, because I lay down My life so that I may take it again.
No man taketh it from me, but I lay it down of myself. I have power to lay it down, and I have power to take it again. This commandment have I received of my Father. John 10:18*

If we only believe these things we would enjoy the same immunity from death Jesus enjoyed. The fallen man is inferior to death. The risen man is superior to death. Most of the Apostle Paul's writings underscores this truth. They were discrete in using the word '*die or 'dying'*. Unless used in reference to the '*old Adamic nature the word* 'D*ie'* is a derogatory word. It is why Apostle Paul preferably used the word, '*sleep'*. As in;

'*For this cause many are weak and sickly among you, and many sleep' 1 Corinthians 11:30*

And Apostle Peter chose to use these words to represent **death**; '*put off this tabernacle'*

Knowing that shortly **I must put off this my tabernacle***, even as our Lord Jesus Christ hath shewed me. 2 Peter 1:14 (Emphasis added)*

It is evident that they consider themselves superior to the spirit of death. They believe life cannot be snatched from them but they only choose to lay it down. Now we see why Apostle Paul say *'For I am in a strait betwixt two, having a desire to depart, and to be with Christ; which is far better:'* ^{Philippians 1:23}

Apostle Paul in this scripture was expressing absolute authority and power over death; he was deciding if he would stay or live. That is impressive! Why would this be surprising to us? If those who live under the Law like Elijah and Enoch did not see death but walked into heaven without the conventional channel of departure, how much more we who live under *a better covenant...*^{Heb 8:6}

I do not really care how serious the illnesses may be it cannot take your life. You will not die, but live to declare the praise of the Lord!

How to lay down our lives Rather than have it taken from us

By making declarations of the mode in which you wish to depart the earth you can create the circumstances by which you exit this earth.

Jesus declared the type of death he was going to die and how he was going to die on at least three separate occasions before his actual crucifixion. He confessed that he was going to go to Jerusalem and that he would be arrested and killed and that the third day he would rise up. Jesus was not sulking. He was engaging the heavenly law. On the cross he said 'Father unto you I commend my spirit' and he gave up the ghost, showing complete control of his exit from the earth. His constant repetition of how he was going to die is not a prediction as many think; it is the putting into action of spiritual laws. Jesus created the circumstances that led to his death.

Everything we enjoy in Christ is always by faith. Nothing falls on our lap by natural order. We have to consciously engage the heavenly life. We live in two worlds. We live here on earth and we also live in heaven. Jesus says we are in the world but not of this world. [John 17:16] We live much the same way an ambassador does; belonging to two nations. One in which he is born and the other in which he serves. Consequently, we observe two sets of rules; Dying is a set of rules in this present world. Laying down life without dying is a rule in the higher world from which we came. In order to lay down your life you ought to engage this heavenly rule by confessing how you choose to leave this earth.

You are going to have to say; for example ' I am going to call my children and tell them of my intention to depart to heaven at so and so age, after giving them instruction, I am going to lay down and sleep and not wake up.' You may choose to disappear like Enoch did. It is your choice. Whatever the choice, you will have to declare it over and over again to empower that heavenly law. Christians need not have their life snatched from them like unripen apples plucked off a tree by sudden wind of sickness, auto accident, or any other catastrophic means. Glory to God! O death where is thy sting? [1 Cor.15:56]

Living seventy years or Forever

If you have given your life to Christ the seventy-year tag life span no longer applies to you. As a matter of fact God never set any seventy-five year age limit. The seventy-five year span arose when the Israelites were dying under a curse. They were dying at seventy years of age. Moses therefore began to intercede for Israel and in his intercession he told God that people were dying too young.

The days of our years are threescore years and ten (seventy years)--or even, if by reason of strength, fourscore years (eighty years); yet is their pride [in additional years] only labor and sorrow, for it is soon gone, and we fly away. Psalm 90:10

As you can see it was not God speaking or setting age limit. It was Moses complaining that people were dying at seventy or eighty -five. Reading in context will show that he attributed this dying at seventy years of age to a curse. Therefore, he interceded for God to remove the curse. A footnote in the Amplified bible makes this clearer.

> This psalm (psalm 90) is credited to Moses, who is interceding with God to remove the curse which made it necessary for every Israelite over twenty years of age (when they rebelled against God at Kadesh-barnea) to die before reaching the promised land (*Numbers 14:26-35*). Moses says most of them are dying at seventy years of age. This number has often been mistaken as a set span of life for all mankind. It was not intended to refer to anyone except those Israelites under the curse during that particular forty years. Seventy years never has been the average span of life for humanity. When Jacob, the father of the twelve tribes, had reached 130 years (*Genesis 47:9*), he complained that he had not attained to the years of his immediate ancestors. In fact, Moses himself lived to be 120 years old, Aaron 123, Miriam several years older, and Joshua to 110 years of age. Note as well that in the Millennium a person dying at 100 will still be thought a child (*Isaiah 65:20*).

There shall be no more thence an infant of days, nor an old man that hath not filled his days: for the child shall die an hundred years old; but the sinner being an hundred years old shall be accursed.

Another amazing promise is even to those under the old testament it is written;

...for as the days of a tree are the days of my people Isa. 65:22

Trees lives longer than humans— some trees lives up to 5,000 years, such as the Bristlecone Pine. Imagine! 5,000 years.

When a man receives abundant life, there is no limit to how long he or she can live on earth. The person can decides how long he or she leaves on this earth as long as Christ tarries.

I came that they may have life and have it abundantly. John 10:10B

Generational Curse hoax

Suppose you are told that your illness is a repercussion of what your parent did or your grandparent did? What would you think? It's a hoax. I want you to know that God has already repealed that curse. God said '*The child will not share the guilt of the parent, nor will the parent share the guilt of the child. The righteousness of the righteous will be credited to them, and the wickedness of the wicked will be charged against them*'
Eze. 18:20 (NIV)

The work of the devil makes us pay for the sins of our fathers; the work of Jesus sets us free from the sin of our fathers. If your illness is a curse originating from your kindred, then you have good news! Just get born-again and all liabilities to your forefathers are neutralized. Jesus Christ is now your Savior and God is your Father. This is how you are freed from the power of curses.

Sometimes we belabor the issue of breaking curses. How do we break generational curse off somebody? We can't! Jesus did already! All we can do is accept what Jesus did by faith.

Christ hath redeemed us from the curse of the law, being made a curse for us: for it is written, Cursed is every one that hangeth on a tree: in order that in Christ Jesus the blessing of Abraham might come to the Gentiles, so that we would receive the promise of the Spirit through faith. Gal 1:13-14

That is the whole reason Jesus came; to break generational Curses. When he died and rose again, God, through Jesus instituted a new family thereby cutting off all spiritual ties to your earthly family. Now you have a new family. Jesus began early in his ministry to let us know a new family is being born.

But he answered and said unto him that told him, Who is my mother? and who are my brethren? And he stretched forth his hand toward his disciples, and said, Behold my mother and my brethren! For whosoever shall do the will of my Father which is in heaven, the same is my brother, and sister, and mother. Mat 12:46:-50

It is fallacy for a Christian to go around finding who to break a curse off of him. I understand that there are times we need help to have faith in what Jesus has done through the work on the cross, If the help goes beyond such assistance in finding that faith then it is not of God. In changing our pedigree through becoming children of God generational curses is broken.

The Bible said, all who did receive him, to those who believed in his name, he gave the right to become children of God. John 1:12 (NIV)

You are now a child of God. Your pedigree has changed.

He is the same, Yesterday, Today and Forever

While religion tells you to believe in blind dogma without questioning, Christianity tells you to taste and see that the Lord is good. Psalm 34:8 Religion thrives on uncertainties Christianity presents infallible proofs... Acts 1:3
For example we don't just tell people that Jesus is alive we provide proofs that he is otherwise Christianity will be another bogus religion doing the rounds. My Spiritual father: T. L Osborn once said if Jesus is alive according to the scriptures, he should be doing the same miracles he did years ago. When we say, Jesus is alive; we do not mean to say he is a ghost. A ghost is never said to be alive.

We are not saying that he reincarnated as a different or new Jesus. He is the same Jesus, yesterday, today, and forever. Hebrews 13:8 Jesus is alive because he rose again after death, and he continues to do the miracles we see. When God raised Jesus up from the grave, He took on higher dimension of authority and power. He could now appear to people supernaturally everywhere even as he appeared to the earlier disciples.

Now Thomas (also known as Didymus[a]), one of the Twelve, was not with the disciples when Jesus came. 25 So the other disciples told him, "We have seen the Lord!"

But he said to them, "Unless I see the nail marks in his hands and put my finger where the nails were, and put my hand into his side, I will not believe."

A week later his disciples were in the house again, and Thomas was with them. Though the doors were locked, Jesus came and stood among them and said, "Peace be with you!" Then he said to Thomas, "Put your finger here; see my hands. Reach out your hand and put it into my side. Stop doubting and believe." John 20:24

Although, the door was locked Jesus was able to come in and showed he was alive. He also proved to Thomas that he was not a ghost. A ghost does not have prints neither can it be touched or heard physically. Jesus is alive!

After his suffering, he presented himself to them and gave many convincing proofs that he was alive. He appeared to them over a period of forty days and spoke about the kingdom of God. Acts 1:3

No religion provides proofs for their teaching. Christianity is not religion; it's not philosophy or something like eastern mysticism. You can experience the power of God now, if you believe in Jesus. If you are sick now and you call on him with all your heart he will heal you, it is a proof that he is alive.

Hospitals are prison cells where people either dies or are released to go back home

I have utmost respect for Doctors. I thank God for numerous hospitals we have across town. Imagine the world without Doctors and hospital! However, we must not forget that God has a bigger plan for the believer when he sent Jesus to die for him. He intended to claim his position as *the Lord that heal us*$^{Exodus\ 15:26}$

Take a look at Jesus ministry, for example, how many doctors did he have on his payroll? None! His healing was not linked to medical science. God wants to heal us and keep us healthy by a higher method superior to curative medicine.

When Jesus talked about opening prison doors, I believe he was talking about spiritual chambers of hell. Hospitals are the physical counterpart of hell where people either die or are released to go home.

"The Spirit of the Lord GOD is upon Me,
Because the LORD has anointed Me
To preach good tidings to the poor;
He has sent Me to heal the brokenhearted,
To proclaim liberty to the captives,
And the opening of the prison to those who
are bound; Isa 61:1

Jesus came to open that prison. A Hospital is just another pool of Bethesda where some people either die waiting, or where Jesus comes and helps get them back home. There are so many unclean spirits that perpetuate illness in hospitals. There are also spirits of death claiming people's lives on a daily basis in hospitals. People may find temporary reliefs, but the hospital remains a section of hell. But thank God, because his hand through Jesus his son does reach out and save even in the hospitals.

*"It's not forgetting that heals.
It's remembering."*
Amy Greene, Bloodroot

CHAPTER 5

OVERCOMING HINDRANCES TO YOUR HEALING

NOW IS THE time to rise above our hindrances and be healed. Whatever the illness may be, just let the Holy Spirit work you through this chapter and by the time you are done, you will be basking in the healing power of God

Faith in what Jesus has done is the Surefire way to healing

It is not what God is yet to do that is going to heal us, but what Jesus has already done. Even if Jesus were to walk up to a sick person now, he would heal him by turning the sick person attention to what happened on the Cross.

Also, healing is not a reward for well-doing. Healing is your heritage. Even as Jesus made us to know '*It is not meet to take the children's bread, and to cast it to dogs.* _{Matt. 15:26} , Clearly implying that healing referred to as bread, is for every child of God. Pleading our nice works before God or subjecting our body to tortuous abuse in the hope of being healed is really faithlessness on rampage. If our healing were to be based on how nice we are, then it will no longer be by grace. There are many nice but sick people out there. Although it is great to be a nice person, in matters of receiving healing, it is standing on what Jesus has done that matters. We must endeavor to understand what Jesus did. Once we understand it, our faith will begin to rise. Understanding of what happened on the cross of Calvary produces the faith to be healed. Jesus stated that if they could understand, they would be healed.

For this people's heart is waxed gross, and [their] ears are dull of hearing, and their eyes they have closed; lest at any time they should see with [their] eyes, and hear with [their] ears, and should understand with [their] heart, and should be converted, and I should heal them. Mat 13:15

I remind people wherever I go that what matters is to understand the gospel. We need to preach and explain the gospel of Christ on the cross so people can understand it. If the work of Jesus is presented so that it can be clearly seen, people will have faith.

Like the case of the Israelites under Prophet Moses, it was looking at the snake on the pole that produced the healing. It is looking at the work of Jesus Christ on the cross that heals the sick. In order to understand, we must bring Jesus Christ on the cross into focus.

..And as Moses lifted up the serpent in the wilderness, even so must the Son of man be lifted up: John 3:14.

A preacher can tell you a bunch of things that are in the bible, but it will not produce healing, unless he tells you about what Jesus did on the cross. Paul said, "For I determined not to know anything among you, save Jesus Christ and him crucified. $^{I\ Cor.\ 2:2}$ Unveiling Jesus on the cross is releasing the power of healing in Jesus name. I have found personally that when I get into studying about Jesus and examining his work on the cross, I begin to experience healing all over my body even in the areas of my life I never thought I was sick. Praise be to his name!

Recounting this story will heal you a confession

Let us hold fast the profession (confession)
of our faith without wavering; (for he is faithful that
promised ;)... Hebrews 10:23

Our confession or profession is a story. It is neither a catalogue of scriptures, nor a blind denial of our medical condition.

When I was very young in faith I used to think that confession for healing means to deny that I am sick. I thought that if I kept saying said "I am not sick" many times enough that the sickness will disappear. I had two people who came to me for help; one was a sixty-year old man with diabetes and the other, a thirty-two year old with AIDS. Of course, I knew no better than to tell them to go and recite over and over again that they were not sick. I was so sure that they would be healed. And when they did not get any better after the confession, I began to wonder what went wrong.

Our profession or confession is an account of what Jesus did on the cross. It is not a statement of denial that we are sick. It is also not a heady repetition of healing scriptures. The way many people have interpreted the word 'confession' leads to a meaningless and mindless repetition of words calculated to bring into effect a cure. They seem to suggest that, by repeating scriptures on healing over and over again like a Hindu mantra, they would make something happen in their bodies. When the awaited change does not happen, they are disappointed and angry at the preacher.

The Greek word translated confession or profession is the word 'homologeo'. It means to agree with what has been done - not only by believing in it, but also saying it. In our case, we are agreeing with what Jesus has done. We are not saying it so Jesus can do it; we are declaring what he has already done. We recount what Jesus has done as an alibi. It helps to know a lot of scripture references with verses, but you really don't have to remember chapter and verses. You don't have to say it in bible language. Men put chapters and verses in the bible. Also, when scriptures are memorized and recited, let it be that we have first understood its meaning and our recital is to the end that we meditate on them. All that really matters is that you can relate to Jesus story on the cross. What Jesus did is an exhibit in the tribunal of life.

Moreover, taking for example the case of confession of sin; it is usually what the person did, not what the person intended. Eastern mysticism does not acknowledge what is already done. By recitation and meditation they intend some force of nature to do something. They speak what they haven't seen in order to see it. We on the other hand, only speak or proclaim what has already happened. Though our optical eyes may not have seen it but through the word of God we see it and believe it.

We having the same spirit of faith, according as it is written, I believed, and therefore have I spoken; we also believe, and therefore speak;' 2 Cor 4:13

For example, you do not need to focus on the cancer in your body. You do not need to deny it is there or keep saying I have no cancer. Just say what Jesus did to the cancer. That is enough. Jesus took cancer away and nailed it to the cross. Forget about the cancer in your body. What do you believe Jesus did to cancer in general? That is what needs to be said. You are saying that Jesus paid the price for your healing. The pain may still be ravaging your body! A thousand voices may be echoing the devastating prognosis within your heart, notwithstanding continue to declare what you know Jesus has done on the cross because it is the truth.

A Demon heard this Story and fled

Dr. Ladonna Osborn the daughter of the renowned world evangelist T. L Osborn was casting out Demons in a church. The demon began to put up a stiff fight. Bishop Ladonna paused and did something remarkable; she said to the demon 'okay listen I am going to tell you a long story,' and she began from the birth of Jesus and went on to tell the story of what Jesus did on the cross. Before she could finish, the demon was completely gone. And the man who had been tormented by the demon was set completely free. Praise the Lord!

Declaration of healing should be aimed at this inner voice of the enemy that seeks to weaken you. This declaration is not meant for people unless they attempt to oppose you. There are healing scriptures both for meditation and declaration at the end of this book.

Do not fight the symptoms fight the doubts

The real confession is saying it out loud enough to drown out this inner defeating voice. It requires courage and if you are not well acquainted with the work of Jesus, it might be difficult to sustain this *combat of words*. It is the doubt that you are not already healed - that you are fighting. This is actually the way to resist the devil; fighting back inner demonic thought of doubt with verbal expressions of the work of Jesus on the cross. These words are the report of what Jesus did on Calvary. They are not mere collection of unrelated Healing scriptures, but a storyline of the work of Jesus on the cross and how it relates to your present condition.

And they overcame him by the blood of the Lamb and by the word of their testimony; and they loved not their lives unto death. Rev. 12:11

Look at those words: '*their testimony*'. Notice it is not in plural as in '*testimonies*'. It is in singular '*testimony*', which means it refers to a particular testimony; the testimony we all have in common, which is the work of Jesus on the cross. If it had said '*their testimonies*' then it would refer to diverse testimonies of so many people. But this Testimony by which we overcame is the work of Christ on the cross.

The words of our testimony defeat the spirit of doubt warring against our spirit. Healing takes place first in our spirit and in our thought. Once the healing is established in the spirit, the spirit transmits the signal to our body. So if you keep looking at your body, you could be deceived and your thought of doubt will increase. The thoughts of doubt manifest as disease; therefore, fight the doubt.

But let him ask in faith, nothing wavering. For he that wavereth is like a wave of the sea driven with the wind and tossed. For let not that man think that he shall receive any thing of the Lord a double minded man is unstable in all his ways...
James 1:6-9

We must hold up our testimony of what Jesus did on the cross as an exhibit, whenever the devil contends our healing. For instance, if you bought a car and somebody accuses you of stealing the car and seeks to dispossess you of the car, what do you do? Do you say oh! I thought this was my car, the car dealers must have lied to me. Do you deny that your car is taken away from you? No! Of course not, all you need do is bring out the title deed and present it as evidence that the car belongs to you. In the same way, what Jesus did on the cross is our title deed; it is the evidence of our healing. And when we do make our confession, we are holding on to our healing that the enemy is seeking to take away from us. We are not a sick person trying to get well we are well persons fighting off sickness; holding on to our healing. Praise be to God!

Mind over matter or the Spirit Declaring rhema

It is important that you receive a spiritual understanding of what Jesus did. In other word, to see the full effect of what Jesus did with your spiritual eyes. Revelation means a disclosure of truth, instruction, concerning things that before were unknown. By the Holy Spirit we can know that which is not obvious. And this is possible when one study's and prays. If you find it difficult to believe or understand what you are confessing; if it appears like a foggy windshield on a snowy day, pause and pray that the Holy Spirit grants you the spirit of wisdom and revelation.

..Making mention of you in my prayer...that the God of our Lord Jesus Christ, the Father of glory, may give unto you the spirit of wisdom and revelation in the knowledge of him: The eyes of your understanding being enlightened; that ye may know what is the hope of his calling, and what the riches of the glory of his inheritance in the saints,
Rev. 1:16, 17, 18

Confession is not mind over matter. It is not the power of sound affecting the human body as in metaphysics. It is not mere power of positive thinking or optimistic visualization like some would make us think. Confession is saying what the Holy Spirit opens your eye to see. Nothing is wrong in thinking positive but this spiritual understanding is more than positive thinking or mental visualization.

Again, the confession springing from Eastern mysticism or metaphysics does not have a person. This confession I am talking about needs an agent; the agent is the Holy Spirit. The Holy Spirit gives us the spiritual understanding of the word we call Rhema word.

Fight mentality, not a victim of mentality

The fight for your healing is in the thought life. These are demonic thoughts attacking the spirit. They are not mere neuron activities in the brain. It is through overcoming doubt that we enjoy our healing in Jesus.

Yet, when this battle is fierce and the sick person is weak, he or she may start getting more demonic thought like *'oh God must have left me'*, *'perhaps I have sinned an unpardonable sin'*. Myriad of defeating thoughts will arise and the person might even start seeing God as the cause of the sickness. All these are demonic thoughts intending to weaken our resolve to fight back. Fight back with your confession. Fight all the way knowing that God is with you.

I once had a vision when I was going through a very tough time. In the vision there was this powerful being behind me. It could have been Jesus, but I was fighting so hard I scarcely was aware of his presence. Then the battle got really tough and I began to turn back, looking up towards heaven demanding what was going on. Just then the being I mentioned earlier, that was standing behind me immediately with a stern countenance turned me around nudging me to continue to fight. He said he was with me and that we don't have any time for whining and that I should keep fighting, he had a stern countenance.

Some people expect to be in the 'ring' and not suffer any blows. The moment they suffer a blow they begin to whine and complain that God has deserted them. That was the case with me. But God said *'fight on, son! Am with you, I am not the one against you. Your whining is really bad now. Fight on to victory.'* Praise God, I was victorious, and you can be too.

Your faith is overly developed in Doctors. What are you going to do about it?

There was a king in those days that started out really humble and he absolutely trusted on God. His name was Asa, the King of Judah. Then he became big and began to depend on his riches - in places where he had once depended on God. As time went on he became sick with what seemed to be cancer of the feet.

The bible said, And Asa in the thirty and ninth year of his reign was diseased in his feet, until his disease was exceeding great: yet in his disease he sought not to the LORD, *but to the physicians. 2 Chronicles 16:12*

But why would he not seek God? This was a man whom when he was yet fragile and Multitude of Army came against him he cried to God and God helped him. Why is it that now he is sick he did not cry to the same God? He could no longer depend on God. He had lost that ability. Over time he had developed his faith in the money he could see and in the best Doctors in town. This is a typical trait; when we have no other hope we cast ourselves at the feet of God. But once we have some alternatives, we are lured away from God.

It is so difficult to trust God to heal your headache when you can just reach up the counter for a box of aspirin, cast two pills down your throat and zap, the headache is gone! It is so difficult to depend on God to fight for you when you have in your backyard a formidable battalion that can adequately contain your enemies. That was the case with Asa. Now he is sick and the best Doctors in town in whom he has become so acquainted and comfortable could not cure him. He could no longer depend on God as before.

In a world where Medical Science is popular, we rationalize *'this must be God in science!'* We say, there are wonder drugs out there and we begin to put too much hope in Science. We are at ease when we should be praying. We are searching through medical journal for the newest method when we should be searching the Scriptures. With the best insurance coverage we cease to call for intensive prayers. This was the case with Asa. His faith was lean in God but fat in the doctors. And that is the problem!

...So he died (of the disease) in the forty-first year of his reign. 2 Chr. 16:13

The reason is clear why he died. Not because God killed him but because *he sought not to the Lord, but to the physicians.* ₂ Chr 16:12 It is not that anything is wrong with Medical Science but it is detrimental to allow faith in Medical science to weaken our faith in God. It's like a god besides the true God. With ground breaking technologies and wonder Drugs, faith in God is waning. To this, we may echo Jeremiah's famous rhetorical question:

"Is there no balm in Gilead? Is there no physician there? Why then has not the health of the daughter of my people been restored?" Jer. 8:22.

It is a curse to be in this situation Asa found himself.

Thus says the Lord: "Cursed is the man who trusts in man and makes flesh his strength, whose heart turns away from the Lord. Jeremiah 17:5

In the name of Jesus, I break every curse off you today, in turning from the Lord to Science. I pray that your faith in God be mightily revived again, in Jesus name. Amen!

Further Note on Medical science

I want to further clarify more on seeking help from Medical Doctors. First of all, I am talking about curative medicine and not preventive medicine or health Care. Secondly, it is all right to seek Doctor's help if your faith in healing through the cross is not well developed. It is the wise thing to do when presented with two evils. You will choose the lesser of the evils. In that case it is better to get the best medical help possible and as quickly as possible.

You may even pray to have access to the best Doctor and a good medical facility. God will answer your prayer as you have decided this is what you want. But there are many cases where the best Doctors and medical facilities are bankrupt of any solution to our problems, what do we do? Very much nothing! That is why we have to learn to develop our faith in Jesus Christ. The higher life in Christ cannot be in operation when the lower life in Science is in force. Therefore, it is important to clarify what type of healing you are seeking; whether medical or spiritual and then proceed to make provisions accordingly. People die because they are on the borderline. God will work according to your faith.

Little foxes, short circuit the power of healing

Confessing your fault one to another removes the blockade that hinder you from receiving healing. In the great passages of faith in the bible, almost certainly, every time faith is mentioned the need to forgive people is always mentioned as well.

It is difficult to walk in hate and walk in faith at the same time. 'Un-forgiveness' is hate. Un-forgiveness is unbelief. Hate or any form of unbelief will short-circuit your faith. Take a closer look at this scripture verses:

*²² And Jesus answering saith unto them, **Have faith** in God... Therefore I say unto you, What things soever ye desire, when ye pray, believe that ye receive them, and ye shall have them.²⁵ And when ye stand praying, **forgive**, if ye have ought against any: that your Father also which is in heaven may forgive you your trespasses. Mark 11:22-14*

You can see here that alongside *'faith'* in verse 22, *forgiveness'* is also mentioned in verse 25. Look also at the passage below and you will find again that faith and forgiveness (or confessing our fault one to another) is tagged together.

*¹⁴ Is anyone among you sick? Let them call the elders of the church to pray over them and anoint them with oil in the name of the Lord. ¹⁵ And the prayer offered **in faith** will make the sick person well; the Lord will raise them up. If they have sinned, they will be forgiven. ¹⁶ Therefore **confess your sins to each other** and pray for each other so that you may be healed. James 5:13-20 (NIV this?)*

When we forgive, we move from the domain of Satan into the domain of God.

We know that we have passed from death unto life, because we love the brethren. He that loveth not his brother abideth in death...1 John 3:14

When we love, our bodies become a receptacle of power. When we hate, we are a repellant of power. The human spirit could be hardened with hate and unforgiveness. I pray in the name of Jesus for a release of the power of forgiveness in your heart. I command that where there is hate, there will be love and tenderness. Declare right now that you have the power to forgive and that you forgive all, in Jesus name and receive your healing.

Demons and false faith: hindrances to healing and how to deal with the demons

There are demonic spirits that parade themselves as the spirit of faith. The idea is to stifle the true faith emanating from the human spirit.

Now the Spirit speaketh expressly, that in the latter times some shall depart from the faith, giving heed to seducing spirits, and doctrines of devils;1 Tim. 4:1

These demonic spirits play on the human mind and make it appear to their victims that what they have is faith, when indeed, their claims are only presumptuous. These oppressed persons, as we may call them even resists medical treatment claiming they are walking by faith. Bear in mind that there is almost nothing demons do not imitate -- from tears, to joy and blowing hot air -- you name it. Demons are all into mimicking everything in order to deceive their victims.

Many years ago, a Friend and I were ministering to a wonderful lady. She seemed to be a true christian. As we began to pray, she fell down like she was under the influence of the Holy Spirit. Had the Holy Spirit not told me she fell under the influence of a pretentious spirit, we would have been fooled. This deceptive spirit feigned the power movement associated with the Holy Spirit so we would stop ministering to her; thinking she was already delivered. We lifted her up and cast the unclean spirit out. Unclean spirits make people enjoy faking power so their victim can be deprived of the true power of God.

In 2002, I ministered to another lady who was being tormented by a sexual demon. When I began ministering to her, she also fell down as though she was under the power of God. She even began to sing songs of praise. This was after three days of continuous ministration. I was elated thinking at last she was delivered! I sat her down and lectured her about Jesus and the need for her to stay focused in the word of God.

When I began to speak these words to her, her countenance changed. Her eyes flushed and became mean. It `looked to me like I was about to be strangled. I knew at once she was not delivered and all the falling down and singing was driven by demonic spirits attempting to prevent her from being delivered. I began to minister to her again, and after three hours, the unclean spirits left her and she was fully delivered -- thank God!

By the heart we guard against demons

In order for us to see the flow of the power of healing, we must do everything from our heart. God is in the heart. The heart is the center of the human spirit. And if we will do what we do from the heart, then we will reach God each and every time we pray.

²² let us draw near with a true heart in full assurance of faith, with our hearts sprinkled clean from an evil conscience and our bodies washed with pure water (Hebrews 10:22).

Electric Properties of the anointing of Healing

The anointing of God is the power of God that we feel. It is the power that is felt coming from either the word of God, or coming from the manifested presence of God. Like the electric field that surrounds a live electric wire, the anointing of God is the power that flows from God and permeates His environment. We sense this anointing when we are indeed praying. We also sense this anointing through the activities of the Holy Ghost who lives in us. (See 1 John 2:27 and 2:20.)

Whether it is felt or not, it is like currents of fire coursing through the body. This anointing destroys problems. It attacks devious and devilish activities in our lives and dismantles them.

And it shall come to pass in that day, that his burden shall be taken away from off thy shoulder, and his yoke from off thy neck, and the yoke shall be destroyed because of the anointing. Isa 10:27

The anointing of God behaves like electricity. The amount of electricity flowing through a conductor is called current. An electric bulb will light up when the amount of electric current is sufficient. If the current is too small, the bulb will not light up. Similarly, if the level and measure of the anointing is large enough to destroy a particular disease, the disease will be destroyed. If it is too little, the disease may not be destroyed.

There is also another measure in electricity called the voltage. The voltage of the anointing is like electric voltage in the natural. It is the degree of force by which the current goes through the body. Voltage is determined by the faith of the individual by which he pulls on the anointing of God. Current is determined by the amount of the word of God working in the heart of the individual.

when you received the word of God, which you heard from us, you accepted it not as a human word, but as it actually is, the word of God, which is indeed at work in you who believe. 1 The 2:13b (NIV)

Also, the more you worship God, the higher the voltage across your body. When a man has undiluted faith, the faith provides a tremendous amount of power to drive the current (which is the word) through the body.

Cancer was electrocuted

I prayed for a lady with cancer once, She was coming to me every week for about three weeks but not much happened. The next time I saw her, I said to myself, I am going to spend more time in worshipping God and praying in tongues so that the voltage will be high enough to drive the current through her body. Now I had been teaching her so much from the word of God in the intervening days. As I said, I did this, so there will be sufficient current of the anointing in her. The current is the amount of power in her, which comes from the

Word. The voltage is the force by which the power goes through her body. The result was different this time. She stopped me in the middle of the prayer exclaiming, 'I am healed! I am healed! It has been many years and she is still healed. Praise be to God!

You can receive God's word or God's power in dosage and if you take in enough dose you will receive your healing. Too many times people receive a tiny little jolt of power and they expect to be healed. When they are not healed, they wonder why?

For they have healed the hurt of the daughter of my people slightly, saying, Peace, peace; when there is no peace (Jer 8:1).

Slight power can only do slight damage to the enemy.

Jesus Ministers higher dosage

And he took the blind man by the hand, and led him out of the town; and when he had spit on his eyes, and put his hands upon him, he asked him if he saw ought. And he looked up, and said, I see men as trees, walking.
25After that he put his hands again upon his eyes, and made him look up: and he was restored, and saw every man clearly. Mark 8:23-25

Notice in verse 25 *'he put his hands again upon his eyes...'* He had put his hands on him the first time, and now he did it the second time. What Jesus was doing here is administering a second dose of the anointing. The first dose obviously was not enough because the man could not see clearly as yet. He saw but a little after the first dosage. The second dose however restored his full vision. If the dosage is not enough, you must take in more!

If donkey talks, and handkerchiefs heal!

I see wonders in God's word: Things that are very difficult to explain, yet very consoling to know. Things like the talking donkey in the book of Numbers. Balaam was set to curse the people of God. But his *ass saw the angel of the LORD, she fell down under Balaam'* and refuse to move forward. *'Balaam's anger was kindled, and he smote the ass with a staff.*

'And the LORD opened the mouth of the ass, and she said unto Balaam, What have I done unto thee, that thou hast smitten me these three times?

And Balaam said unto the ass, because thou hast mocked me: I would there were a sword in mine hand, for now would I kill thee.

And the ass said unto Balaam, Am not I thine ass, upon which thou hast ridden ever since I was thine unto this day? Was I ever wont to do so unto thee? And he said, nay. Numbers 22:27-29

The ass is not really a talking beast. God's power came upon the donkey and its mouth opened to talk. It saved her master from death; who apparently did not see what the Donkey saw. I also see through the word of God that handkerchiefs from Apostle Paul were able to retain the Power of God - sufficiently enough to cause sick bodies to get well.

*And God wrought special miracles by the hands of Paul. So that from his body were brought unto the sick handkerchiefs or aprons, and the diseases departed from them, and the evil spirits went out of them. Acts **19:11-12***

How amazing! Handkerchiefs and aprons are only inanimate objects, but they were able to carry the power of God. Also, the Shadow of Apostle Peter radiated the power of God as well. Think about it, a shadow is really nothing but a shade created when light rays are blocked. But it was able to heal the sick. The point in all of these is that if a Donkey receives power, Handkerchiefs and shadows retain power, not to mention the burning bush and staff of Moses both of which had the capacity to release the anointing of God, what do you think of the human body? I think the capability of the human body to manifest, hold onto, and release the power of God is unfathomable.

What do you think of your Pastor or anybody praying for you? Should you not expect a greater degree of the power of God from such a person? You can get caught up in the nitty-gritty of who is fit to heal or minister to the sick, or who is holy or not holy enough that you lose your blessing! Sometime ago, a certain man of God came to minister in our Church. It was later found out that he had so many unpleasant stories in his docket. Certain people then came to me asking if they should discard all the godly expectation they had from his meeting. I told them that we must uphold all our expectation and that though his character may stink but God will still perform the words

He had spoken through him. I said if God could speak through a Donkey, which by a long short is neither holy, nor noble, He could certainly speak or heal through anybody who spoke His word.

Anointing Conductors

In the study of electricity, materials that carry electrical current are called conductors. The ones that do not are called insulators. It is the same in the spiritual arena. Things that can carry the word of God are anointing conductors. It seems to me that the rod of Moses, the staff of Elijah, and the donkey of Balaam were conductors. Even handkerchiefs and shadows were also used as carriers of the anointing. If these things can retain the power of God sufficiently to effect healing, think of the capability of the human body. What a super conductor! That is why the woman said if *'I could touch the helm of his garment (I know the garment is a conductor),'* speaking of Jesus garment, *'I will be made whole.'* Mark 5:28

If we lose confidence in the ability of God to use people, we may never get healed because God uses men and sometimes, unlikely men.

... Believe in the LORD your God, so shall ye be established; believe his prophets, so shall ye prosper
2 Chro. 20:20

Anybody who believes in the power of Jesus enough to pray for you is a conductor. He commands the uncommon power of God. It is a prophecy being fulfilled when a hand is laid on you. That hand is electrified.

..they will lay hands on the sick, and they will recover." Mark 16:18[c]

Alter your thought, Aid the power that flows

When you alter the way you think about your minister, it alters not only the amount of power that flows from him to you, but also the way the power flows to you. The woman with issue of blood believed in Jesus. She believed also that Jesus' cloth was electrified with power. Jesus was being thronged by the crowd but *Jesus said, Somebody hath touched me: for I perceive that virtue is gone out of me.* ^(Luke 8:46) At first it seemed ludicrous. His disciple asked why he would say somebody touched him when there were a crowd of people thronging him.

'Peter and they that were with him said, Master, the multitude throng thee and press thee, and sayest thou, who touched me? Luke 8:45

The truth is that, though many were touching Jesus, only the woman with the issue of blood pulled power out of him. She was not caught up in the euphoria of the moment. She believed even the clothes of Jesus could heal and it healed her. Some other people believed that Jesus had to touch them before they can be healed, and it was like that unto them as well. Yet there are those who believed that Jesus only had to speak the word of power and they will receive healing, and that is exactly what happened; according to their faith. Your faith in your minister plays a significant role in aiding the power transfer for your healing!

Act on the word

One can have the kind of believe in God that only amount to *question-asking*. Gideon asked; *'Oh my Lord, if the LORD be with us, why then is all this befallen us?* ^(Judges 6:13) Such faith does not have much power. It may eventually lead to God's response. Another person can believe God, but his or her belief may only serve to the extent that this individual only have mere hope, in which case he or she continues to expect. Indefinite expectation may console, notwithstanding, it will never lay hold of God's promises.

Thirdly, one can believe enough to act on the word of God until result is achieved. Such a person is a *'now'* person. Faith is yesterday, now and forever. it is never later. There is no such thing like I have faith now, but the result comes later. Result of faith is now. This is because faith is an eternal event. That is, the event we are expecting has already happened; it is happening; and is forever happening. faith is always an outcome of what has been done already. Therefore one has to believe that no matter what it looks like on the outside, the miracle has already happened. In other word, one has to act immediately. Only those who believe enough to act on it have the faith necessary to effect a miracle.

When Apostle Peter prayed for the cripple at the gate, the man did not immediately experience healing. It was when Peter acted on the word by helping the man up, that power came into the man's leg.

Then Peter said, "Silver or gold I do not have, but what I do have I give you. In the name of Jesus Christ of Nazareth, rise up and walk. "And he took him by the right hand, and lifted him up: and immediately his feet and ankle bones received strength. And he leaping up stood, and walked, and entered with them into the temple, walking, and leaping, and praising God Acts 3:7-8

It is true that the power of God may be fully at work to heal you; yet, you may not see any visible manifestation of that healing until you have acted upon the word of God upon which your faith is resting.

Faith is consummated when you take a step in the direction of what you have prayed for. We need not wait for a clue to see if God has healed us. When Peter was done praying for the cripple, 'he *took him by the right hand, and lifted him up'.* Exercising yourself is your responsibility not God's!

Kenneth E. Hagin's testimony

When Kenneth E. Hagin, a renowned faith preacher, got healed on the bed of paralysis as a little boy, he still could not get off his sick bed the following morning. He knew he was healed but he had not experienced anything in his body, the following morning God spoke him *'Hagin, if you were healed why are you still laying down?'* Then, he tried getting up but it was very difficult, believing that God already healed him; he continued to make effort to get up.

He held unto the rail, pulled himself up inch by inch, edging himself to the side of the bed. It took him over an hour just to sit up. But that was when he began to experience the power of God in his bones. Exercising his faith paid off. He finally was able to stand after more than two hours of trying, and he was completely healed. Exercise your faith now if you know you are healed. Glory be to God!

In tough and desperate times when your creativity begs to be birthed, loose the confines of the ground; stand up in your faith and walk atop the waves
— Stanice Anderson

CHAPTER 6

TESTIMONIES OF HEALING THROUGH THE WORD

The word of God is like an embryonic plant. It is in a state of arrested development until it enters the human heart. Supposing the heart provides ideal condition for growth, the word sprouts into a growing phase; self-preserving and self-propagating it matures in the heart. When it matures it not only alters the state of the man

but it destroys tough old foreign bodies that wages war against his health.
The Word of God is light. It is a self-advancing energy of enormous radiation in the human soul able to burn off even the finest print of disease plaguing the body.

Fibroid Disappears during the teaching of the word

Ms R. was invited to one of the meeting in which I was ministering. We were not praying, this was in January 2008. I was just doing some teaching on the name and the power of Jesus. When she came in I observed that she looked about six months pregnant.

The following day she testified that God had healed her of fibroid in the meeting. She said her belly, which was protruded was not pregnancy but fibroid. She said during the teaching. She felt the power go through her and she instantly felt her stomach flatten. Praise be to God!

Where the word of a king is, There is power

I was telephoned by a Lady who had been suffering from ulcer for many years. She had times when the pain would be really severe, she called during one of those times. So I told her to get her bible, I opened her eyes to see some of the things I have been teaching in this book. Namely, that diseases obeys us when we speak. Then I spoke to the ulcer to heal up. Right away the power of God went through her body. Now it is important to quickly add that after the word of authority was issued there was no visible or external clue that anything had really happened.

Since I knew she had been healed, in order to demonstrate her healing, I asked her if she had anything hot or spicy in the house. I told her to have a full meal of whatever the spicy thing was immediately. She did and no pain or symptoms of ulcer that usually trouble her anymore. She was healed. I continued to see her in Church and three years afterwards and she was still giving her testimony.

She chose to stay and her Cataract was healed

It was a Saturday evening Service, She and her daughter walked into our prayer conference meeting. After sitting for a while they found out that they were not in the meeting they had planned to be. The daughter suggested they leave but the mother decided they stay.
In the middle of prayer this exchange took place. I had seen them walk in and sit at the back.

When the meeting was over just about the time I was getting ready to make announcements, she asked if she could give a testimony. She said she had almost lost her vision to cataract. She has been back and forth to the Doctors for the past seven years. She testified however that while prayers were being offered, she felt scales falling from her left eye and, now, she could see perfectly.

It is amazing that God healed her of cataract when nobody was praying about cataract nor did anybody know if anybody had cataract that day. You see God knows:

Every little tear drop you shed
Every little headache inside
He cares; he really, really cares for you

What happen is that she came under an atmosphere heavily laden with power. And she got healed.

Skin cancer healed after word radiation

Ms A. has been attending our teaching meetings for several weeks when in one of the meetings she found that something had happened in her body. In most of these meeting all I do is teach the word of God. I scarcely ask anybody what their problem is. Not that I did not care, but the nature of the meetings does not allow for that. I therefore did not know if she had any of such problems.

The following day after one of the meeting she went to see her Doctor and the Doctor told her, apparently after some examination that some changes have occurred. She later testified to the glory of God that her skin cancer was completely gone from that moment.

Often we are told to be very detailed about our needs; otherwise, God would not answer us. Sometimes, however the word of God is not sniper-precision it could also be like a cannon shot that blows up anything in its path when it is released with the power of the Spirit. When we are exposed to the atmosphere of God's great power, it is not a matter of how detailed we are about our needs. I believe it has much to do with God's grace and mercy. God just wants to touch and heal our sicknesses and diseases.

I have given a few of these testimonies in order to illustrate the power of the word of God. The Word is all sufficient, all knowing and all that we need. The full blast of the gospel will heal anything and anybody. *'For it* is the power of God unto salvation to everyone that believeth; to the Jew first, and also to the Greek' Rom 1:17

How God healed me of chronic illness
Several years ago

My Parents did not know Jesus Christ when I was born. They sought help from native Doctors or juju priest as some people call them. I was born with a chronic illness and was constantly suffering from fainting spells - always in and out of hospitals. The *Juju* priest recommended some rituals for my parents, which they practiced until they met a group of Christians from the Assemblies of God Church who introduced them to Jesus Christ. My mother became saved, and began to be more courageous as her faith grew in her heart to trust God for my healing. The native Doctor or *Juju* priest had warned that unless she continues to practice those rituals, I would die. In fact, I had many near death experiences and my illness was atrociously unbearable.

Though, I did not recover from the problem but my parents received enough spiritual strength to discontinue the rituals.

Four years later when I was about sixteen years of age, a Lady introduced me to Jesus Christ. My mother brought me to the Church, and a young Lady named Yemisi Foluhi led me to Christ. She gave me a book written by Oral Robert on healing. After I read through the pages, I came to trust the Lord, and trust that as a believer I could no longer be bound by sickness. I was excited about my new found faith and I went everywhere telling my friends that I could not be sick anymore. However, it did not take long and I became ill again. I was very discouraged, and I wondered why I should be sick after I had found Jesus? I could not make sense of what was happening in my life. Soon I regained my health

After reading the scriptures on healing through Jesus Christ, I was fired up. Again, I began to tell my friends I could not be sick - that it was impossible for me to fall ill. It was not long after my confession that I fell ill and my friends rebuked me. They concluded that my boasting had contributed to my frequent illness. They said I should stop talking about Jesus and divine healing. I was ashamed and discouraged. I believed the word of God about healing, but I just could not figure out why I was still sickly. When I again regained my health, I boasted again that I will not be sick anymore.

......Again, for the third time I fell ill and was bed ridden. I was mocked and scorned. The trend must have occurred two more times. Each time, I would get better, and confess I could not be sick again. But the sixth time, I got better and Praise the Lord, I was never sick again! I went on several years not knowing what pain or headache was, nor do I now. I was completely healthy. This was such a big deal for my parents who were exceedingly grateful to God.

I don't really know what term I should use – stubborn faith or child-like faith, but through faith in Jesus Christ I was made whole. My genotype reads AA Now. Glory to God!!

*If you follow reason far enough it always
Lead to conclusions that are contrary to reason.*
-Samuel Butler

CHAPTER 7

CONCLUSION: FIVE ESSENTIALS TO MIRACULOUS HEALING

Look to Abraham your father and to Sarah, that bare you: for I called him alone, and blessed him, and increased him....Isa 51:2

The life of Abraham provides excellent summary of faith for healing. God so rejuvenated Abraham that at hundred years of age he was able to impregnate his wife. God healed Sarah's womb and renewed her body too. There are five things that must happen in order to receive a miracle. We see these five things play out in

the life of Abraham who is given to us as an example of faith.
1. Prevenient visions
2. Planted visions
3. Professed visions
4. Persuaded visions or promise
5. Praises to performance of miracle

Prevenient visions or desires

For he gave them their own desire; Psalm 78:29

God is the one that gives us the desires we are having as the text above suggests. When Abraham desired to have Children, his desire for a child was not only appropriate; it was a God-ordained desire. How else was God going to make a nation out of him according to his promise; '*I will make of him a great nation...*$^{Gen\ 12:2'}$?

Far before Abraham began to desire a child God knew he was going to bless him with one by his wife Sarah. God always start his work in us far before we are aware of it. What he does however is to legitimize the thought as ours by placing objects directly in front of us to the end that they will point us in a direction. Every cry of man for miracles is a manifestation of the breadth of God's desire. These desires can be called prevenient visions. The Old Testament stories are prevenient visions for us to desire the miraculous. They suggest the work of Jesus in advance; God both supply and fuel our desires by the Old Testament prophecy and stories. Your desire for a miracle came from God. And any unbelief is a counter devilish action against miracles. Sometimes we think our desires for a miraculous healing is stupid or unrealistic. That type of thinking limits the force of our pursuit. As the Lord said 'what *things soever ye desire, when ye pray, believe that ye receive them, and ye shall have them.* ^(Mark 11:23)

The beginning of a miracle is desire, as evident in Abraham's desire for a child.

And Abram said, Lord GOD, what wilt thou give me, seeing I go childless, Gen 15:2

Once we have this God-given desire such as your desire for healing going the next thing is planted vision.

Planted vision

Look up at the sky and count the stars…Genesis 15:5

The second thing is that God plants a vision in us. We see what others can't see. God took Abraham outside and said, "Look up at the sky and count the stars—if indeed you can count them." Then he said to him, "So shall your offspring be. Once God planted that vision in him Abraham no longer had a mere desire for the miracle, he saw himself in the miracle and he saw the miracle in him. It is at this point that we identify with the miracle. These visions produce a very strong unquenchable conviction. The bible declared that after this vision *Abraham believed.* He saw the invisible and believed. This is what God did when he lifted Jesus on the cross and demands that we look. Even as those who looked at the serpent Moses lifted up in the wilderness were healed so the vision of Jesus on the cross will heal us.

After we have been implanted with visions we will begin to profess.

Professed of vision

Neither shall thy name any more be called Abram, but thy name shall be Abraham; for a father of many nations have I made thee... As for Sarai thy wife, thou shalt not call her name Sarai, but Sarah shall her name be... **Genesis 17:5**

Here is where some Christian gets stranded. They wonder why their believing is not working. They would say 'I believe yet nothing is happening' or "I believed and nothing happened" , 'is God's word true?', ' What have I done wrong?' We should remember that when Abraham believed it was great and definitely a step further in his quest for a child. He, however did not get the child until well over 14 years later when he began to profess it. This is the third step to the miraculous. It is professing what we see. God told Abraham and his wife to start acting as father and mother rather than barren. God told them to talk their faith. It is in saying what you believe and saw in the vision that you release your faith. God showed Abraham a vision, he then change their names to conform to the vision. Abram is now called father of nations (Abraham), and Sarai is now Sarah; *'she shall be mother of nations'.*

Unless we have a change of name we cannot have a miracle. Each time Abraham tells people his name, he tells them I am 'father of nations'. And I can imagine the people wondering 'he does not even have a child'. As it is evident, this is not mere optimism. God also commanded us to do the same thing; 'let the weak say I am strong'. We believe what Jesus did therefore we speak. Whoever is in need of healing today is essentially in the same situation as Abraham was in those days. Abraham was childless; he was called father of nation when he was yet without a child. All he had was the word of God. The word he had is *'so shall thy seed be'* He refused to consider neither his wife's dead womb nor his own senile body. He continued to declare that he is a father of nation. It may not appear you are healed. All you have for now is the word of God that says 'you are healed by his stripe' God is asking that you to call yourself 'the healed' When we pray for people they already healed even before we pray for them. All they need do now is 'nomenclature', that is, a naming ceremony. You are now 'the healed' however hopeless that sounds.

'Persuaded visions' or promise

And being fully persuaded that, what he had promised, he was able also to perform. Rom 4:21

There is a difference between believing and knowing. Abraham first believed, and then he became persuaded, that is he knows now. When he believed it open doors to more spiritual exploits but the child was yet elusive. After fourteen years plus when he became fully persuaded the miracle of the child only took a year. To know is to be fully persuaded. This is the third step to the miraculous. At this point your profession has opened you up to the divine spirit. It is no longer you now it is God in you.

Abraham who against hope believed in hope, that he will become the father of many nations, according to what was spoken, so shall thy seed be. (not according to his feeling), he was not weak in faith, he considered not his own body now dead, when he was about an hundred years old, neither yet the deadness of Sarah's womb: He staggered not at the promise of God through unbelief; but was strong in faith, giving glory to God;

And being fully persuaded that, what he had promised, he was able also to perform. [Rom. 4: 17-21]

Another thing to make a note of is that he has completely abandoned himself to God. The scripture declared that he hoped against hope. That is, in the natural, without God and God alone it will be impossible. This is the hardest and the darkest times in the quest for miracle, but by the spirit of God it is possible to completely abandon ourselves to God. As long as God is one of the alternatives to healing there will not be a miracle in view. When he hoped against hope, that is to say that all hope was gone. All he had left is what had God said; *'so shall thy seed be'* [Rom 4:18b]

I must emphasize that I don't mean that we trust in God in a general sense as many people do, when they seek help from different sources believing that God is in all. Miracle is God and God alone.

Praises to performance

He staggered not at the promise of God through unbelief; but was strong in faith, giving glory to God And being fully persuaded that, what he had promised, he was able also to perform. Romans 4:20-21 KJV

Perhaps, this is the single most important step you can take. In this all elements of faith can be manifested. Praising God is what we do when we have done all and in order to do all that is required for miracle. Abraham was praising God because God's word was real to him, he praised God because he saw it in a vision, and he praised God because he was fully persuaded. He praised God because to him the miracle was done.

I pray for you today for visions, persuasion and strength in Jesus name.

BLESSING TO OTHERS

As this book has been a blessing to you be a blessing to others by helping pass this book around to those you think need the Gospel of Our Lord Jesus Christ. We will also appreciate if you can write us or leave a comment on our website to let us know how this material has been of help to you.

Mark Asemota Applied Gospel for Global Outreach. MAAGI Inc. www.MAAGI.info

Healing Scriptures for Meditation

In the following order read, meditate, understand, memorize (if you can) and recite any of the following healing scripture in your quest for divine healing and health.

1. I will put none of these of these diseases on you, I am the lord that heals you. Exo 15:26

2. I will bless your bread and water and take sickness from your midst. Exo 23:25-26:

3. I shall let no evil befall you, neither shall any plague come near your dwelling Ps 91:9-10:

4. I the Lord heal all your diseases, redeems you from destruction; and renews your youth like the eagle's. Ps 103:1-5

5. I the Lord saves you out of your distresses. And heal you and deliver you from destruction. Ps 107:19-20

6. I will not put on you none of the diseases of Egypt and I will be your physician Exo 15:26

7. I the LORD will take sickness away the midst of thee. Exo 23:25

8. I will let None of you have miscarriage in your pregnancy. Neither shall you be barren. Exo 23: 26

9. I take away from thee all sickness, and will put none of the evil diseases of Egypt on you Deut 7:15

10. No evil will befall you, neither shall any plague come near your dwelling. Ps 91:9-10

11. My Word is medicine and health to your flesh. Prov 4:20-23

12. I the Lord Surely he hath borne your grieves, and carried our sorrows and I was wounded for your transgressions, I was bruised for your iniquities: the chastisement of your peace was upon me; and with my stripes you are healed. Isa 53:4-5

13. As you Fast before me I God will cause our health to spring forth speedily Isa 58:6-11

14. I God will restore health unto you again. and I will heal your wounds, Jer 30:17

15. But unto you that fear my name shall the Sun of righteousness arise with healing in his wings; and you shall go forth, and grow up as calves of the stall. And you shall tread down the wicked; for they shall be ashes under the soles of your feet Mal 4:2-3

16. Ask, and it shall be given you; seek, and ye shall find; knock, and it shall be opened unto you: Matt 7:7-11

17. I the Lord heal all the sick and delivered those possessed of devil. Matt 8:16-17

Say what Jesus did

18. Jesus healed every kind of disease and sickness in all villages and cities about all the cities and villages Matt 9:35

19. Jesus healed blindness, paralysis, and the mute, multitudes came unto him, having with them maimed, and many others Matt 15:30-31

20. God anointed Jesus of Nazareth with the Holy Ghost and with power: who went about doing good, and healing all that were oppressed of the devil Acts 10:38

21. The Lord heal and do signs and wonders in Jesus name Acts 4:29-30

Personalize these Healing declarations

22. Every mountain will moves at my command in Jesus name. Mark 11:22-24

23. I have power over devils and sickness in Jesus name Mark 16:17-18

24. Jesus heals my brokenheart, delivered me from captivity and recover my sight and set me at liberty, Luke 4:17-19

25. I have Command over all devils, and to cure diseases. Luke 9:1-2

26. I have a mandate to heal the sick everywhere Luke 10:8-9

27. I am a child of Abraham I cannot remain bound in Jesus name Luke 13:16

28. God heals and even cast out devils even through the Shadows of his servant Acts 5:15-16

29. Christ hath redeemed me from the curse of the law, being made a curse for me: for it is written, Cursed is every one that hangeth on a tree: Gal 3:13

30. The prayer of faith shall save me from sickness, and the Lord shall raise me up; and if I have committed sins, they are forgiven me now. James 5:13-16

31. And this is the confidence that I have in him, that, if I ask any thing according to his will, he hear me: 1 John 5:14-15

More Healing Scriptures

32. I the Lord wish above all things that you may prosper and be in health, even as your soul prospers. 3 John 2

33. I the Lord makes the barren woman abide in the house As a joyful mother of children. Psalm 113:9

34. Sing, barren woman, you who never bore a child; burst into song, shout for joy, you who were never in labor; because more are going to be your children...says the Lord Isaiah 54:1

35. Then God remembered Rachel, God gave heed to her and opened her womb God can never forget me therefore. Genesis 30:22

36. 'Behold, I will bring health and healing; I will heal them and reveal to them the abundance of peace and truth (Jeremiah 33:6 NKJV)

37. Come, and let us return to the LORD; For He has torn, but He will heal us; He has stricken, but He will bind us up. Hosea 6:1 NKJV

38. Have mercy on me, O LORD, for I am weak; O LORD, heal me, for my bones are troubled Psalms 6:2 NKJV

39. O LORD my God, I cried out to You, And You healed me. Psalms 30:2 NKJV

40. I shall not die but live, and shall declare the works and recount the illustrious acts of the Lord. Psalm 118:17 Amplified Bible (AMP

41. And if the Spirit of Him Who raised up Jesus from the dead dwells in you, [then] He Who raised up Christ Jesus from the dead will also restore to life your mortal (short-lived, perishable) bodies through His Spirit Who dwells in you. Romans 8:11 Amplified Bible (AMP)

42. For though we walk (live) in the flesh, we are not carrying on our warfare according to the flesh and using mere human weapons. For the weapons of our warfare are not physical [weapons of flesh and blood], but they are mighty before God for the overthrow and destruction of strongholds, [Inasmuch as we] refute arguments and theories and reasonings and every proud and lofty thing that sets itself up against the [true] knowledge of God; and we lead every thought and purpose away captive into the obedience of Christ (the Messiah, the Anointed One), 2 Corinthians 10:3-5 Amplified Bible (AMP)

43. [Not in your own strength] for it is God Who is all the while effectually at work in you [energizing and creating in you the power and desire], both to will and to work

for His good pleasure and satisfaction and delight. Philippians 2:13 Amplified Bible (AMP)

44. For God did not give us a spirit of timidity (of cowardice, of craven and cringing and fawning fear), but [He has given us a spirit] of power and of love and of calm and well-balanced mind and discipline and self-control. 2 Timothy 1:7 Amplified Bible (AMP)

45. He personally bore our sins in His [own] body on the tree [as on an altar and offered Himself on it], that we might die (cease to exist) to sin and live to righteousness. By His wounds you have been healed. 1 Peter 2:24 Amplified Bible (AMP)

46. Casting the whole of your care [all your anxieties, all your worries, all your concerns, once and for all] on Him, for He cares for you affectionately and cares about you watchfully. Be well balanced (temperate, sober of mind), be vigilant and cautious at all times; for that enemy of yours, the devil, roams around like a lion roaring in fierce hunger, seeking someone to seize upon and devour. Withstand him; be firm in faith [against his onset--rooted, established, strong, immovable, and determined], knowing that the same (identical) sufferings are appointed to your brotherhood (the whole body of Christians) throughout the world. 1 Peter 5:7-9 Amplified Bible (AMP)

47. You will live a long life. With long life I will satisfy you, And show you My salvation." (Psa 91:16 NKJV)

48. You can take authority over the sickness in your body. "Assuredly, I say to you, whatever you bind on earth will be bound in heaven, and whatever you loose on earth will be loosed in heaven. (Mat 18:18 NKJV)

49. You can find strength in God and His Word "…. Let the weak say, 'I am strong.'" (Joel 3:10 NKJV)

50. Jesus has already paid the price for your healing. who Himself bore our sins in His own body on the tree, that we, having died to sins, might live for righteousness; by whose stripes you were healed. (1 Pet 2:24 NKJV)

51. Can the prey be taken from the mighty man, Or the captives of a tyrant be rescued?" 25Surely, thus says the LORD, "Even the captives of the mighty man will be taken away, And the prey of the tyrant will be rescued; For I will contend with the one who contends with you, And I will save your sons. 26"I will feed your oppressors with their own flesh, And they will become drunk with their own blood as with sweet wine; And all flesh will know that I, the LORD, am your Savior And your Redeemer, the Mighty One of Jacob." **Isaiah 49:25**

www.ingramcontent.com/pod-product-compliance
Lightning Source LLC
Chambersburg PA
CBHW050558300426
44112CB00013B/1978